Best wishes.

THE EVOLUTION OF A TEACHER

An eyewitness account

Don Edgers

DON EDGERS

authorHOUSE®

AuthorHouse™
1663 Liberty Drive
Bloomington, IN 47403
www.authorhouse.com
Phone: 1 (800) 839-8640

Published by AuthorHouse 02/02/2016

ISBN: 978-1-5049-7748-7 (sc)
ISBN: 978-1-5049-7749-4 (e)

Print information available on the last page.

Any people depicted in stock imagery provided by Thinkstock are models,
and such images are being used for illustrative purposes only.
Certain stock imagery © Thinkstock.

This book is printed on acid-free paper.

*I am dedicating this book to all the teachers,
and especially my colleagues, and students
in whose presence my life was spent.*

CONTENTS

ACKNOWLEDGMENTS

Special thanks to:

My wife, Carolyn, for her tireless encouragement, suggestions and patience with me as I slogged along in this undertaking.

Daughter, Eryn Jackson, and grandson, Phoenix Raye, for listening and responding to readings I did while constructing this tome.

Son-in-law, Mark Jackson, for his computer help in preparing this book.

My high school classmates, Bob Mack and Tom Kruse, for reading and commenting on segments of this book while it was in progress.

Students I especially liked and appreciated – I don't particularly like to label students, because of possible embarrassment, as "Teacher's Pets," but the fact is there are many students who made my time in the classroom productive and worthwhile. My *teacher assistants* (TAs) need to receive kudos from me for keeping me from becoming swamped with paperwork, running errands, supervising, and just generally helping me from sometimes being overwhelmed.

I can't remember the names of all these helpers except those who went way over and above the tasks I entrusted to them – Dusty C. in Media Now and Film Study. Eric R. was another assistant who went beyond the expectations of a TA during the gas shortage days and drove my car to get in line at a station near our school in order to get gas. Dawn D. wasn't my assistant, however, she took many a load off my shoulders by helping me with after school chores.

- *Student Body Presidents* who were dedicated to their position and who were leaders of note are Butch H., Anna C., and Greg G. All three have remained in contact with me.

- *Outstanding Drama and Speech students* are greatly appreciated and fondly remembered because of all the time we spent together. Butch H., Craig S., Phil C., Linda R., Bill H. and Rob S.

- *Film Study/Film Making & Media Now students* who demonstrated outstanding creativity and shared their abilities and creativity are: John G., Jeremy M., Dave A., Eric & Nels R., Tom H., Sandy C., David P.

- *Yearbook/Video Yearbook students* tended to go over and above their assigned duties and are often unmentioned for their dedication to a year-long task that most of the student body appreciated. All those involved deserve mention, but I'll only mention the editors: Tersa K., Lou L., DeMaris C., Ann A., Jeremy M.

Interior Graphics/Art Credit: John Mikkelborg

INTRODUCTION

This book is an attempt to chronicle a segment of life that generally lasts 12 or 13 years in most Americans' lives – *school*. High school normally occupies 1/3 of this time, however, in my case high school lasted 34 years - four as a student in a military school ('53-'57) and thirty as a teacher - 28 in public, two in private ('67-'97).

I believe most of *my* life's abilities, experiences and circumstances were aimed to my eventual 30-year occupation. This book will explain how I arrived at this conclusion.

There must be a DNA marker (gene) for probable occupations. My paternal grandfather and father were dentists; Grandmother and a great aunt were teachers. On my mother's side of the family Grandfather, was a minister, Grandmother was a music teacher and Mom taught high school for two years. So, my gene pool menu reads: 4 teachers – 2 dentists – 1 minister.

For most of my early years and through high school, I told everyone who asked me what I wanted to be when I grew up was that I wanted to follow in the footsteps of my dentist father and my grandfather (although being an explorer, archeologist, railroad engineer, or sailor had entered my mind) but *never* the thought of becoming a teacher. Nevertheless, all those wished-for occupations never occurred and I became something I didn't wish for – a teacher.

As a historically-oriented writer, I want to preserve my memories of 60 years within the 20th century relating to students, teachers and schools. I've endeavored to write these personal classroom memories in an interesting manner.

Whereas I don't claim to have a highly superior autobiographical memory (*hyperthymesia*), my recall of many people and events is very good. The views expressed in this book are mine, and may differ from others in the same place and time. Recently (2015), a writer-classmate of mine (class of 1957) upon reading my memories of our time together said, "Are you sure we went to the same school?"

I've changed some names, but not necessarily the events. There are some judgements I've made concerning teachers, colleagues, students and administrators which sound harsh/critical because at the time that's the way I felt. I have since realized that I failed to consider the biblical admonition to "Judge not, lest ye be judged"; the American-Indian proverb, "Never criticize a man until you've walked a mile in his moccasins"; (or if I appear hypocritical), "Why worry about a speck in your friend's (students', teachers', administrators') eye when you have a log in your own?"

If my presentation somehow makes me sound boastful, forgive me. I am mainly amazed and appreciative that I managed to hang on though many bumps in the career path I pursued. Obviously, as you read on, the smooth and rewarding times outweighed the bumps in the path I chose.

FOREWORD

~Changes~

It is interesting, and sometimes unbelievable, to look back at how much school, society and attitudes have changed during the span of my 76 years. The 50 years I spent in classrooms (13 years in K-12; 7 years in college; 30 years as a teacher) is like a study of the Dark Ages to the Age of Enlightenment.

Blackboards became green; white chalk became yellow; chalkboards were replaced or supplemented with overhead projectors and eventually became white boards using colored markers. During the time of chalk and erasers, well-behaved students were often excused from class to take the erasers outside of the school building and bang them together to get rid of the embedded chalk dust. Sometimes several eraser 'dechalkers' would get together and see who could make the biggest chalk-dust cloud and become invisible. We certainly weren't invisible to our mothers when we got home and were greeted with, "What in the world have you been doing that's covered you in white dust?"

In my early years, school desks had holes for inkwells built into their tops, although in the 1940s we no longer used dip pens. There were stories of when inkwells were still being used that little boys sitting behind a girl with pigtails would be overwhelmed by the temptation to dip a tail into the well – especially when the hair being dipped was blonde. We did, however, have liquid ink pens with built-in little rubber bladders that with the aid of a small lever on the side of the pen sucked ink from ink bottles students stored within their desks. Liquid ink had a tendency to smear (especially for left-handers) so blotters were needed. The preferred ink colors were blue, black and blue-black. Ballpoint pens started being used after WWII, and tended to let little blobs of ink to be randomly deposited on the paper which couldn't be absorbed satisfactorily with a blotter, so got smeared or transferred to the writer's hands and shirt sleeves.

Typewriters were manually operated with an ink ribbon that was either all black or ½ black and ½ red and generally the font was Times Roman

12. When electric typewriters made it into schools in the '60s, fixed fonts were replaced with typing balls that could be rotated to one of four different sizes and styles of fonts, and it was no longer necessary to manually scroll the paper on a roller. The sounds of the manual and electric typewriters was markedly different, and there was no longer the sound of a bell to alert the typist that the end of a line was fast approaching.

Advances in technology & effects on teaching

[1949] *Handwriting* was the only way we could use to make books for a 5th grade project.

[1956] *Ditto* machines were used to publish a bi-weekly newsletter for our high school.

[1957-61] Transcripts were *handwritten* at the University of Washington for all student records and. coursework tests were *dittoed*.

[1962] The first time I had to produce multiple copies for lessons was in Japan where I taught English conversation and colloquialisms to medical students and medical research students at the University of Hokkaido. Copies of the lessons were produced on a *manual typewriter* using carbon paper and only five copies at a time could be typed (actually pounded) out for 15-20 students. I did this for two years.

[1963-64] A monthly report from our military post to others throughout the world was accomplished via a *teletypewriter* that was used to send typed messages from point to multipoint over various types of communications channels.

The teletype was adapted to provide a user interface to mainframe computers. Realize that mainframe computers were in their prehistoric phase of development, requiring large rooms to accommodate their bulk. Mini and micro were not used in the same context with computers. Our WWII-vintage teletypewriter was housed next to the computer room and would create a punched tape (like a tickertape) for onsite printing or transmission. This was all well and good *until* the electrical current to our building was changed from 60-cycles to 50-cycles. Suddenly, the printouts became bipolar, resulting in the printing of figures that didn't make sense. The computer couldn't compute! My work section had to manually make our reports balance before sending them out.

[1967] ***Photocopiers*** were in use in the school district, but used sparingly because there was only one machine for the entire district and each teacher had to prepare their own masters and operate the machine, which was located in the district administration office building, at odd times, usually after school.

[1970s (version 1.0) ***Xerox photocopier.*** With the Xerox machine next to my classroom, it was very convenient for me to make personal copies, but with the convenience of the machine came the responsibility of maintenance: cleaning, keeping the toner and toner oil levels full. When word got out to the other schools in the district, more and more teachers came to my realm, and the machine got more and more usage. The machine started showing signs of old age, and the Xerox repairman spent a lot of time keeping it running. By looking over his shoulder I received on-the-job training for repairs. Eventually, the poor guy was overwhelmed and probably took to drinking, because of our battle-worn copier. Anyway, *I* became the repairman. As the copier aged, and when it didn't operate properly, especially when teachers from other schools used it, I would frequently be interrupted during my classes for requests to fix *my* machine. I began to keep a log of the time spent on the machine, submitting a bill to the principal at the rate of $10/hour. Surprise, surprise, I couldn't be reimbursed, but could get comp time, which I didn't want. I submitted my refusal to do any more repairs and maintenance, and suddenly, somebody was hired to do the copying. Eventually a new photocopier replaced the veteran Xerox and it was moved out of my building to a building near the Administration Buildings. Eventually, our school buildings had their own copy machines, and the Administration Building copiers printed larger print jobs.

PART I

AS A STUDENT

~1~

Grade School

.

Role Models

"I am always ready to learn, but I do not always like being taught." Winston Churchill

<u>KINDERGARTEN</u>

In my five-year-old brain I regarded Kindergarten as a benchmark of an awesome educational experience. Our legendary teacher, Miss Entz, reminded me of a mother hen with a gruff voice. When asked by adults how I liked school, I could honestly say I loved it – at least everything but naptime. I think only one or two kids actually slept, and they had just returned to school after recovering from some debilitating childhood ailment. I would have much preferred to play, listen to a story, or see a movie - but nap?!

We kindergarteners lived in our own little world with our own toilet, and a play court separated from bigger kids by a four-foot cyclone fence bordered by a thick hedge, except for a padlocked gate leading out to a playfield inhabited by big kids and where we weren't allowed to venture. I recall one day when a big kid came to the gate and told us, "Never put dried beans up your nose or dried peas in your ears." After giving this advice, he disappeared into the throng of revelers on the 'forbidden' playfield.

At the age of three, similar advice from my oldest brother was given when I was admiring a rabbit cage containing rabbits in the open trunk of a car that was about to leave. I was warned not to hold onto the bumper of the car when it drove off. I had never thought about doing such a thing *until* he said it. I was able to keep up with the car for a short distance, but ended up being dragged along behind the car until my arms gave out and I skidded down the road, passing out from the pain of the skid. Several weeks later most of the scabs had disappeared.

FIRST GRADE

I think I was at the top of the dumb kids' list, way back in first grade when we were learning to read. As we progressed in our *Dick & Jane Readers*, I made it up to the fast reading group even though I couldn't read! Somebody who *could* read would always read before I had to recite. The 'actual' reader would say, "Look, Look. See Jane jump. Jump, Jane, jump!" I simply repeated what the person before me said, only a little faster. — Then, the day came when *I* had to read first.

When I admitted to one of my older brothers that I couldn't read, he said, "You know the alphabet, don't you?

"Yeah."

"Do you have some bubble gum comics?"

"Yeah. I'll go get some."

After retrieving a handful of the comics, which I previously had only looked at the pictures, my brother had me sound out the words, and within a short time, I'd mastered reading. Because my brothers had read some of their *Classic Comics* out loud to me, I was able to figure out bigger words and surprised my teacher, my classmates and myself when I took on new pages in *Dick & Jane*.

I really wanted to be a smart kid, but didn't know how to become one. I knew of classmates who just seem to *get it* right off the bat. You know, the kids who raise their hands immediately after, and sometimes before, the teacher asks a question. My first experience with someone like that was in first grade. His name was Tommy, and if he hadn't been so short he would have been promoted to sixth grade because of his intelligence. Sometimes I'd watch him when we had an assignment to read something and then answer the questions. The class of 24 'average' students might spend 30 minutes completing an assignment. Tommy wouldn't crack open his book until our teacher said, "Class, you have five minutes to complete your assignment." He'd read the assignment and be finished by the time Teacher said, "Time's up!"

SECOND GRADE

Second grade was a real eye opening experience because my 2nd grade teacher was my first experience with a genuinely compassionately-challenged aka 'mean' teacher.

The school year promised to be special: World War II was over, and because my ancient school building was overcrowded, I would be in a portable classroom located only a few steps away from the school's playfield and isolated from the noise and general hubbub of the main building. Little did I know that what I thought would be wonderful situation would turn into a 'bad dream.'

While eagerly working on a craft project with nubbins of leftover prewar crayons which were kept in Lucky Strike cigarette tins, it was necessary to ask fellow classmates if their tin might have a coveted and rare black color. Young kids can't draw most pictures without using the black color first. Suddenly, our teacher clapped her hands and announced, "Class, you're making too much noise. Noisy students are naughty boys and girls." With a scary witch-like voice she hissed, "I want it so quiet that I can hear a pin drop." Magically, a pin appeared between her thumb and forefinger. The pin dropped— we held our breath, remained as still as possible, and strained to hear. All eyes were on our teacher as we awaited her verdict. "I'm sorry children. I didn't hear it," and with a Mona Lisa-type smile continued, "I'm going to have to punish you."

My stomach started to ache because I didn't know how or if I would be punished. The girl behind me, the same one who threw up on the kid in front of her in first grade, started whimpering. The teacher, who had been opening a drawer in her desk, turned her attention to the whimperer, bellowing, "SILENCE! – or it will be all the worse for everybody." She dramatically and slowly withdrew a ruler from her top desk drawer, abruptly closing it. The ruler was held much like a policeman might hold a Billy club as she dramatically strolled down the center aisle of the classroom. "Look straight ahead and place your hands on top of your desks! I will walk down each aisle and punish the noisiest boys and girls." I wondered if the recipients of her wrath would be struck on the head, face or hands. A loud slapping sound, followed by a yell of pain or fright filled the room! Bladders emptied, and sphincter muscles tightened. Time slowed, and my ears began ringing. I closed my eyes as another slap and yell rang out. When the eternity of punishment was over, we all resumed breathing – quietly. Kindergarten and first grade had introduced us to bullies and mean kids, but a mean teacher, who held us hostage in the classroom several long hours a day, was a dreadful new experience. Several times throughout the year, we'd be denied recess because of one student's 'naughty' behavior. The antagonism we developed toward our tormentor seemed counterproductive as some rebel seven-year-olds with a death wish, threw spit wads, made noises or created other distractions when Teacher's back was to us. As time went on we spent more recesses inside as even some of the meekest students contributed to the brief bursts of mayhem.

About mid-year a 5th grade teacher, who held title to being the "meanest teacher" in our school, brought a boy from her room in the main building to our portable in order to humiliate and punish the supposed n'er do well. Apparently, he hadn't done what was called 'homework' or had committed some other unpardonable sin not appropriate for a 5th grader. The trip to our portable was more likely a tactic to strike terror into our hearts in order to imprint her 'coveted' reputation into our minds. The large red-faced boy had a runny nose and was unceremoniously pushed into a front row desk that was too small for him and told, "Put your head down and don't raise it until I return." From my desk I could see strings of snot that slithered from his nose and hung down like transparent snakes, almost touching the desk. He would suddenly snuff them back into his nose, playing with his 'snakes' while he endured his time in our concentration-camp portable.

Toward the end of our teacher's reign of terror, she pulled a new tactic. After roaming the aisles, she announced, "Class, I can smell that somebody needs a bath." Judging from the amount of shuffling and shifting, several of us may have fit into that category. She made her way down my aisle, sniffed each of us, stopped in front of me — backed up, and looked at the boy in front of me.

"Roger, I think *you're* the culprit."

"NO, I don't need a bath!"

"Did you take one yesterday?"

"Well, no, but I don't need one."

"Do you want the class to decide?"

"No."

"I'm calling your mother, and if she's home, you're taking a bath."

Our classmate protested while being dragged from our room.

Normally, if our teacher left the room, all hell would break loose; however, on this occasion we were absolutely dumfounded by this act of supreme humiliation. It was possible to feel the overwhelming frustration. The whimpering girl behind me started weeping, and most of the rest of our class put their heads down on their arms and let the tears flow. At the age of seven I vowed that if I became a teacher, I would *never* be like our second grade teacher.

THIRD AND FOURTH GRADES

A Wise teacher makes learning a joy — Proverbs 15:2

Third and fourth grades had good teachers. In fact, my fourth grade teacher would get my vote for the most positive teacher in the world. This lady was encouraging, good natured, interesting, and knew how to get the most out of her charges. For example, when I did something stupid, instead of labeling me "dumb" she would suggest how I could improve my performance.

George Bernard Shaw must have had me in mind when he said, "A man (boy) learns by staggering about making a fool of himself; indeed, he progresses in all things by making a fool of himself." For example, the boy who sat next to me, was a very fast reader who would emphasize his skill by slamming his book shut when completing the assignment. He would sigh and lean back in his seat with his hands behind his head. Then he'd look at me with a smug look on his face. I couldn't stand it! The next time we had something to read, I'd look out of the corner of my eye to see when I thought he might be ready to slam his book shut, I slammed mine shut just before he did. The teacher knew I hadn't done the reading and that we were having a book slamming showdown, so said, "Boys, when you're finished reading, leave your books open, then go back and reread the lesson until I say the time's up. Not everyone is as fast as you, and the extra noise is distracting. O.K.?" She didn't shout or scowl. She gently admonished us and made us think.

Although I didn't realize it at the time, she handled awkward situations tactfully. We had a girl in our school who could be classified as having a touch of Asperger's. Someone discovered that she could quickly spell any word you gave her. Her performance when spelling Mississippi was very impressive, plus she gave the spelling a little added twist by spelling, "Capital M – I – double s – I – double s – I – double p – I." One recess the girl caused a crowd to gather around her on the playfield, not based on her spelling ability. Looking like a fight had developed, our teacher hustled to the group, and discovered the fast-speller standing in the midst of the mob – bare naked! The teacher, who had an interesting dilemma, sprang into crowd control. The girl was told to put on her clothes while the onlookers were told to disperse. When the girl was clothed, our teacher took the girl's hand and walked her back to school. Somebody had serendipitously discovered the fast-speller would take off her clothes if she was asked. After that day, the girl never graced our school again.

Thank you, Mrs. Waddel.

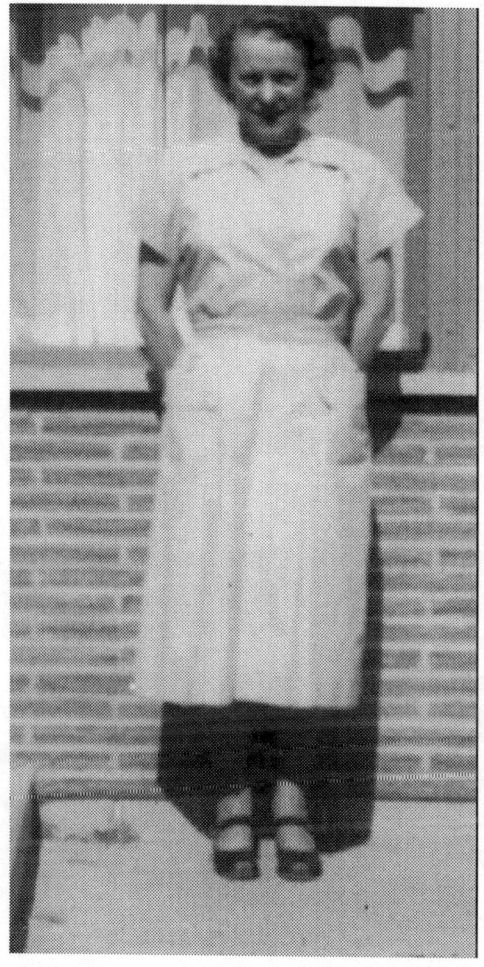

My 4th grade teacher, Mrs. Waddel

<u>FIFTH GRADE</u>

*"The secret to education lies in respecting the
pupil"* – Ralph Waldo Emerson

In fifth grade I got the school's "Meanest Teacher." Just the thought
of having this teacher made my eyes tear-up, and my stomach
would be in knots at the recall of the boy she had brought into my
second grade classroom three years earlier. Actually, she was a good

book knowledge-type teacher, but seemed to lack compassion or understanding of student motivation.

When we would have spelling competition, she cut no slack for the weak spellers, and forced them to try spelling difficult words. I recall an *Archie* comic book where the football coach was trying to get a mentally-challenged player qualified in English in order to play in the upcoming game. All he needed to do was get one letter correct in spelling the word 'coffee.' He spelled it K-A-W-P-H-Y.

One of the girls in our class, who nowadays would be classified as 'Special Education,' would almost have a nervous breakdown when forced to spell. Once, she wet her pants while attempting to spell. When the pee puddle was pointed out to our teacher, the girl was told to go to the girls' lavatory clean herself up and stuff paper towels in her underwear. Upon the girl's return, her dress was sticking out like a ballet dancer's tutu. Of course our teacher berated the girl for doing something beyond her understanding or mental capabilities. Everyone in the class felt bad for the girl except our teacher.

One day, one of the 'weaker links' in our classroom, a boy, suddenly stood up and asked in a loud voice, "Who said that?" It was possible to hear the groans of our class members because we knew our teacher would light into this kid like a starving dog on a meat bone. And she did.

"Jerry, what's the matter?"

"Somebody said they were going to get me." I was close to where he made his accusation, and heard nothing.

"Who said it?"

"I don't know, but I heard it."

Our teacher lectured us for about five minutes about threatening others, which, because of her actions and earned reputation, went in one ear and percolated in our minds in order to work out a way to get her goat. Eventually, we realized we had a classmate who we could drive nuts – and we did. It only took us about a week to cause the poor kid to drop out of school for a while, and demonstrate to our teacher we could overcome her weakness of human understanding. Kids can be mean, too.

The antitheses to my mean teacher was the other 5th grade teacher in the school. I seem to remember she had white hair, and a ready smile to match a twinkle in her eye. She spoke kindly to all who greeted her, and was looked up to and admired much like a celebrity because she had invented a travel game that a game company supposedly bought. She also was the leader/coordinator for the school's elite movie squad of three or four students that set up and showed classroom movies. One showing in the kindergarten room was a film I'd seen when I was in that room, *"The Tortoise & the Hare."* Evidentially the film had not been replaced with a new copy, because there were so many splices in the film that the tortoise moved at a supersonic pace, and the hare was in a time warp. I also observed a little boy and girl making out in the darkened room. Romance at age five?!

During recess one day a boy I had known for a couple of years, and was in my Cub Scout Den, came up to me and handed me a quarter, saying, "Here's 25 cents for you." I thanked him and kept it, thinking he was doing his good deed for Cubs, because when we'd meet, the Den Mother would ask us if we'd done any good deeds. I was pretty conscientious about carrying packages for Mom, holding doors for people, and always looking for the allusive old lady to help across the street. My 'paying friend' continued giving me a quarter every day, and when I refused it, he would force me to take it by putting it in my pocket. Finally, in frustration, I asked, "Why do you give me a quarter every day?"

"To be my friend."

"You don't have to pay me to be your friend. I'll be your friend for free. Don't give me any more quarters." He stopped giving the coins to me directly, but found ways to put them in my school desk, lunch pail when I brought lunch, and my jacket pocket.

I also got a job during lunch selling milk, so any hot lunches I got were free. Pop gave me $1.25 every week to buy hot lunches, and I'd forgotten to tell him I was getting free lunches. Sometimes I'd spend five to 15 cents after school at the bakery or soda fountain, but my income accumulated faster than I spent it, so I had to deposit it somewhere. Throughout the weeks I'd stowed my coin cache in different drawers in my bedroom. One day when Mom was putting clean clothes into one of the drawers she stumbled upon about $10.00 or $20.00 worth of coins. I happened to be nearby when she spotted them and I heard her let out a little gasp like she'd seen a spider. "What in the world are all these coins doing in this drawer?" she asked as she piled the coins on top of the dresser. Being a relatively honest kid, I told her about my windfalls. She really got upset with me and told me that Pop would no longer give me lunch money and that I had to return every cent my friend had given me. I hadn't wanted my friend's money in the first place and I hadn't spent any of his quarters, plus I didn't spend money for much of anything, so my life wasn't going to change at all. "I don't want to ever see these quarters in this house again!" said Mom in an uncharacteristically stern tone of voice. I put the offensive coins in a lunch sack to return to my school friend. Mom hadn't discovered the other coins that I had put in the bottom of a cigar box I used for crayons and pencils. I covered the coins with a folded sheet of paper, then put my crayons and pencils on top. I felt a little guilty about doing this, but I'd heard enough details about the Great Depression that made me realize that people who had cash at home were better able to survive when banks closed. I looked upon the hidden money as an emergency fund.

When I handed the sack of quarters to my paying friend I said, "My mother told me I had to give back these quarters, and if you give me any more quarters I won't be your friend."

"I won't take back what I've already given you, but I'll quit giving you quarters to be my friend if you're not going to be my friend," he said with a hurt look on his face. "But will you still be my friend?" "I told you a long time ago I'd be your friend without you paying me. In fact, after school let's stop at the soda fountain, and I'll buy you a malted milk, a milk shake or a banana split and maybe some comic books. Okay?"

We stopped at the soda fountain in a drug store after school and I managed to spend a few of my friend's quarters. I asked the soda jerk if he'd give me paper money in exchange for the rest of the coins in the sack, and he agreed. I had not followed Mom's warning about returning with the coins, and added the paper money to the coins in the bottom of the cigar box.

SIXTH GRADE

Sixth grade gave us a teacher for each subject. We were exposed to a variety of personalities, teaching styles and abilities of those who lorded over us.

I succeeded splendidly as a mediocre student in my aspirations in the classroom setting. I earned the moniker "smartest of the dumb kids" from my 6th grade homeroom teacher when I became lazy in doing homework. I thought I had psyched-out my teacher and volunteered answers at the beginning of the class, with the thought that the teacher wouldn't call on me more than once. Also, sitting at a table near the back of the classroom with one of the "dumbest" helped my cause of achieving near invisibility to our teacher.

Mrs. J. was my homeroom teacher, a lady who had good potential as a teacher, but failed to understand that some students just don't have what it takes to succeed academically. Case in point: At my table of three was a boy, a year older than most of his other classmates, who was dyslexic. Back in 1951 the general public didn't realize that some students who were labeled stupid, actually were dyslexic. I think, though, that this boy was doubly cursed: ignorant and dyslexic. Why Mrs. J called on him to read made me and most of my classmates question her wisdom as a teacher. We would universally groan when we'd hear, "Would you read the next sentence?"

"Do I hafta?"

"Yes, you do."

Our table of three was near the rear of the room. The third person was a cute girl who made my time with the "repeater" tolerable, especially when we'd have bomb drills and we had to crowd underneath the table. Her smile would make me oblivious to the complaining and cursing of our outcast tablemate.

Before making his attempt at reading aloud, he would inevitably offer up cursing and swearing in a low voice at the teacher.

"The -, the boy -, the boy who –"

Mrs. J. would repeat her never-changing admonition – "Just read the complete sentence. Quit backing up!"

Before continuing his fruitless attempt, he'd emit a stream of curses, causing those of us within earshot to snicker.

"What did you say?"

"The boy who stood -, the boy who stood up -, the boy who stood up, pushed –"

Mrs. J. would finally give up and have me read.

"The boy who stood up, pushed the chair into the wall."

He would grumble and curse me for showing off, while our female table companion read the next sentence.

Mrs. J. just didn't get it.

I had an art class that I enjoyed. The unmarried teacher was slightly scary because the white parts of her eyes were yellow and she was wont to frequently emit a loud "Shhht!" sound when we got a bit noisy. Other than that she demonstrated her ability to teach and encourage even the lamest artist in the room. A friend of mine didn't share my enthusiasm for art. One day he dared me to call the teacher a whore. Having never heard that word before and being naive to the mischievous bad intentions of this "friend," I uttered this new word to the instructor. The response I got was something else. Rather than lay into me verbally, she simply said, "What?" Like the 6th grade idiot that I was, I repeated the "word." She calmly escorted me to the hallway, closed the door, and asked me if I knew what the word meant. I timidly muttered, "No." She then asked me who put me up to asking and I quickly gave her the name of my so-called friend. The "friend" got chewed out royally, and never again dared me to do or say anything.

Math has never been my strong suite, but I can do it. Our math instructor proved to be a total dud, who lacked the ability needed to encourage or teach. We simply went over lessons in the book or did speed drills for addition, subtraction or multiplication ad infinitum. I learned more mathematics at home from my mother, who briefly taught the subject after graduating college. There was no attempt to instruct, and even our uneducated minds understood the meaning of lazy.

Male role models were nearly absent in my elementary school. The exceptions: the principal, the janitor and a 6th grade teacher.

- The *principal* was a stern man, who seemed unable to smile or laugh. I knew that to be sent to his office was not desirable, although I only had two occasions to interact with him. Both times involved the same boy, a neighbor, who had a slight mean-gene and a talent to goad, who tested my patience with ill thought-out consequences. In other words, he pushed his luck. When we were in 3rd grade he pushed my head down on a water fountain, chipping one of my teeth. I took out after him as he ran down the hall to the principal's office. The principal chewed me out for chasing my antagonist, and simply told him to quit pushing my head down on the water faucet.

On a walk to school after a nighttime snowfall, there was slushy snow on the sidewalks and grass parking strips, which my companion scooped up and packed into slush balls to throw at me. After doing this two or three times, I told him to knock it off. While holding a slush ball in his hand, he asked, "What are you gonna do if I throw this one? I said, I'll punch you in the nose. He threw the missile, and I punched him in the nose, causing it to bleed just short of needing a transfusion. The bleeding was stopped with a handkerchief. When we arrived at school, bloody-nose-boy waved the "red flag" in front of the teacher and whined, "Donnie punched me in the nose!" All three of us took a brisk walk to the principal's office for a little talk. The principal, remembering our previous meeting, commented, "We meet again. What did you do this time?" I was advised to bring any problems I had with my neighborhood nemesis to the teacher, rather than strike when the iron was hot. It was obvious the principal didn't know my neighbor boy as well as I did, and the only way to deal with him was to react quickly and decisively. This principal managed to dog my tracks throughout my entire first eight grades even though I went to three different school buildings. Although he spoke numerous times at school assemblies, the only thing I recall him saying in understandable English was, "If you wear out the eraser on your pencil before you wear out the lead, you're making too many mistakes!"

- The school's *custodian* was an affable middle-aged man who mostly kept to the school's coal-fired furnace/boiler room. Once in a while he'd come out of his lair to clean up a spill or attend to discipline-related problem with us boys. One time he showed up in the boys' lavatory when we were in the midst of having a long-distance peeing contest. We would see who could stand the farthest from the urinals and get the pee in. Of course, our endeavor made the floor a near-wading pool of pee which got tracked from the lavatory into the hallway. The normally soft-spoken janitor made his displeasure known to all present, with a warning that if it happened again, he knew each boy present, and we would clean up the mess and be reported to our parents. Guess what never happened again?

Every day after lunch he would stand by the garbage cans with his large dust mop in hand seeing to it that we cleaned up after ourselves. Observing how much wasted food got thrown away, it was arranged to have all uneaten food and milk to be gathered and displayed on a lunch table. Every classroom was brought to the lunchroom to see how much food we wasted in one day and told statistics of how many people in the world starved to death.

- My *first male teacher* taught science and P.E. I recall that in a P.E. class he raced a speed-demon 6th grade girl in a 100-yard dash, and SHE won! The only thing I remember about the science class is one of my oddball classmates furnished garter snakes for display in a waterless aquarium. I tended to be nice to eccentrics, and was interested in what they did, so one day after class the odd classmate wanted to show me his latest contribution to the aquarium. As he was peering into the tank he exclaimed, "It's not here!" We frantically looked around the tank and on the floor for the missing snake, to no avail. As he looked back into the snake's glass prison he thought that one of the reptiles looked suspiciously fat. He invited me to watch him perform an operation on the slightly obese critter. I declined the invitation which turned out to be fatal for the snake, and fruitless in producing the missing snake. After the "operation" the teacher asked the snake aficionado to keep his serpents at home.

He said he would pay me 50-cents to come to his house to see his collection of garter snakes. Nobody else was willing to see his menagerie for any amount of money, and I probably could've held out for a dollar, but I sort of felt sorry for him because he didn't have many friends at school or in his neighborhood. We also belonged to the same Cub Scout pack, so I was reminded of the Scout motto: Do a good deed, daily. I figured it would only take a little while and he'd be happy that anybody wanted to see his snakes, and my good deed was worth 50-cents. After I beheld and handled all five of his garter snakes, I was paid off. I told him I'd picked up lots of them on Fox Island, which excited his interest, and he told me he'd pay me 25 cents for every one I brought to him.

As I was about to leave, 'snake boy's' three-year-old brother came upon the scene and big brother said, "This is my little brother, and he is a genius. He has memorized the record labels of every 78 rpm record in our large record collection!" The records were stored in sleeves in albums that held 15 records. There were 50 albums or more. Taking an album off the shelf and opening it to the fourth sleeve he said, "Little brother, what's the record label say for album five, record four, side B?" As I looked at the selected record label, and without hesitation, the little boy said, "That is Columbia record A2699 and does not have a denotation for side A or side B. One side 78273 is *When You Look in The Heart of a Rose* from 'The Better 'Ole' by Florence Methven, sung by Charles Harrison. The other side, 78270, is *Salvation Lassie of Mine* by Caddington and Story, sung by Charles Harrison. I was flabbergasted! This little kid could spit out the information as fast as a machine gun, and I had a hard time seeing some of the information he was giving. I had no idea a record label contained so much information. I wondered if the brothers noticed my mouth hanging open and my look of astonishment. Before I could close my mouth, the little genius said, "Record five in album five is a Brunswick record, 3037-A is for dancing the Fox Trot, titled *A Little Bungalow*, from 'The Cocoanuts' by Berlin performed by Harry Archer and His Orchestra. I love that one!" He hummed a bit of it then said, "3037-B, also for dancing the Fox Trot is called *Great Big Bear* Introducing '*Vodka*' from '*Song of the Flame*' by Harbach, Hammerstein, Gershwin and Stothart, performed by Harry Archer and His Orchestra, and the record's price in the US is 65-cents, but in Canada 85-cents because of the exchange rate." I had no idea what this little kid was talking about, and the more he performed the more stupid I felt. I had a little four-line poem to recite at a Mother's Day Assembly at school that I spent the better part of two weeks trying to memorize and when it came time to recite it I could barely remember one line. This little boy sounded like an adult in a child's body, and I had suspicions that "child genius" was snake-boy's father who actually was a midget. As I extricated myself from the basement with the excuse that I had to get home, I felt like I had gotten paid to go to a circus sideshow.

I'm unclear about how students were picked to have the prestigious and coveted job of hall monitor, but I do remember being one. Students were not allowed to be in halls during class time without a hall pass. What the penalty for failure to produce one was I don't recall, and I only remember one time when I challenged a student who came barreling out of a classroom with a panicked look on his face. "Where's your pass?" I challenged. His quick reply while on the run – "I'm going to throw up – where can I go?" The lavatories were one flight down, but there was a mop closet close by – to which I pointed. The sick student quickly opened the door *next* to the mop closet and threw up in a classroom. The astonished teacher, in an angry voice, demanded, "What's the meaning of this?!" Sick boy, pointing to me, exclaimed, "He told me to!"

To be selected to be on the school's movie squad was one of the highlights of my grade school years, because I thought I might achieve some admiration and respect from my peers I wasn't able to achieve in sports, music, art or academics. I was able to acquire a skill most students and teachers couldn't or didn't want to master. When needed, I would be called upon to set up the movie projector, thread it, show the film, rewind it, and return the equipment to the movie equipment room. Movie projectors didn't change much over the years, so I was able to use my skill for another 50 years in schools, community and church meetings and even in business when training films were shown.

We had assemblies for various reasons, but usually so teachers could have their skills as directors of dramatics or music be displayed by students interested in these indoor activities. The school's music teacher somehow managed to get students to be able to read music and play instruments – usually girls playing violins or other stringed instruments – pretty much in unison. It was rather awful sounding, but I sort of respected their courage to show off their newly acquired ability to an audience.

The librarian of our local public library would periodically come to our school to promote new books throughout the year, and near the end of the school year to recruit those who enjoyed reading into a summer reading program. If the enrollees read at least eight books, they would be rewarded with a certificate. I think most of our teachers read to us throughout the year, so, many of us liked to read for pleasure. Storytelling skill is to be admired, and our neighborhood 'library lady' exhibited an ability that would put a used car salesman to shame. After one of her presentations kids would practically break their necks running to the library to check out books. When we had completed our goal of reading eight books, we would be quizzed on two or three of our books, and if she was satisfied, be checked off. Those who successfully completed the required reading were presented certificates at a school assembly.

Occasionally we were treated to field trips. Teachers had to demonstrate their crowd-control abilities, especially with those in our midst who had designs of disruption at any cost. The word "don't" translated to "do" in the brain of a potential anarchist-rabble-rouser. Short trip-control of students when visiting cookie or potato chip plants was easy, because good behavior had a tangible reward. More difficult were trips to a ballet/acting demonstration, newspaper tour, and a Coast Guard icebreaker tour. The most difficult crowd-managing challenge was in 5th or 6th grade when most of us went to the foot of the Cascade Mountains to stay overnight for several days in military-style barracks. We learned firsthand about the flora and fauna, first aid, conservation and safety in the wilderness. We even planted seedling fir trees in a logged off area alongside a major east-west highway where we could watch our trees grow over the years.

Sixth grade classmates - 1951

~2~

Junior High School

Junior high (grades 7 & 8) teachers, as a group, are to be admired, if for no other reason than the ability to put up with beings who can't concentrate or remain still for more than a few moments at a time and who have the emotional stability of psychotic kangaroos. If hormones emitted an odor, it would be overwhelming to most adults; however, most eighth grade instructors found a way into our pimply exteriors and our still-forming brains. I think the only exceptions to the above might have been gym teachers. Gym teachers at that level seemed to have bypassed or scored low in their psychology classes.

Gym was actually torturous to immature, physically underdeveloped, socially handicapped, and plain uncoordinated kids. Gym teachers have physical interests and abilities, but seem to lack the compassion gene. All boys are NOT created equal! So who does the teacher attract? - The natural athletes and physically fit kids who love physical activities and competition.

My summer activities of rowing and tree climbing really aided me in gym class when I went back to school in the fall. When we had to climb ropes, I managed to get up and down before most kids could get up. Chin-ups was another area where I did well. Another activity we engaged in, boxing, called for my rowing arms' strength and endurance. Boxing was big in the sports world in the 40s and 50s, and even I, the least interested-in-sports person, knew the names: Joe Louis, Ezzard Charles, "Jersey" Joe Walcott, Rocky Marciano, Floyd Patterson, et al. My newly-built junior high school in Seattle decided to include boxing as an activity and establish a new tradition of featuring the best boxers in gym class in a boxing match. The gym teacher informed us that the top boxers in three different weight classes would perform and compete in an upcoming smoker. I let my gym teacher know that I didn't like to box so that I wouldn't have to compete. Since we weren't on the best of terms, he assured me in a demeaning way: "You don't have to worry, because you don't have the stuff it takes to get through the preliminaries." Unfortunately, for me, I discovered I had the ability of doing something I didn't want to do. I managed to block my opponents' blows and found a way to score blows in return. The gym teacher's astonishment was matched equally by my sparring partners — and me. When the smoker arrived I was to fight in the middle-weight category. My opponent turned out to be my best friend and the YMCA Golden Gloves Boxing Champion of 1949!

Fellow classmates, including the kid appointed as my second, expressed condolences and sucked air through their teeth like they might at the sight of seeing a dog about to be run over by a car. All bets were on my opponent, with odds of 100 to 1 against me! When I approached my boxing buddy I appealed to our friendship and implored, "Please, don't beat me too badly!"

"Don't worry, I'll take it easy on you. Just dance around a lot," he reassured me with a wink.

In an entry in a diary I kept that year I expressed my anxiousness about the whole situation. I was as nervous as a lame dog in a room full of clog dancers. The lightweight match was first, and ended in a draw. When my match was announced, I wished I'd thought about relieving myself before entering the ring. My second talked some calm into my tense-state, and I recalled my opponent's advice to "dance around a lot and advised, "Keep your guard up!" My opponent danced around with me for the most of the first round, occasionally striking out. I didn't attempt a single blow, and didn't receive any. When I got to my corner, I was congratulated for fending for myself, and then was advised: "Every time he swings at you, he drops his guard. This round keep your guard up, and when he swings and drops his guard, give him a hook or uppercut. You'll score some points." Early in the round, he swung at me. I blocked his blow, then nailed him with a hook and knocked him down! The raucous yelling suddenly ceased and from the stunned onlookers a few "Geez's" were uttered. We had been instructed that if we were knocked down to stay down until the eight-count, but the boxing champ was up and swinging by the three-count. His reputation was now at stake, so he had to put me in my proper place as quickly as possible. He was a man with a mission and kept up a frenetic pace of swinging, though ineffectively, to the end of round two. I'd obviously won the round. My second slapped my back with a painful congratulatory thump, saying: "See, I told you! All you have to do is keep your guard up, and keep him moving, and you've got it made. Don't let him get you in a corner, either." I was apprehensive about the final round, but followed my second's advice, and also managed to get in blow or two when 'the champ' attempted to score a punch in my direction. The final round would probably be judged a draw. It was, but because I'd made a major score in the second round, I had my hand briefly held up by the astonished gym teacher and was declared the winner!

In the locker room I encountered a discouraged, and soon-to-be, former best friend sitting on a bench with his head hung down. I tried to boost his morale, but was unsuccessful, and we didn't speak much to each other ever-after that fight. The only other person who seemed to be happy about my victory was my dad. In the following days practically anybody who'd witnessed my victory told me how lucky I'd been, and some challenged me to a fight. A neighbor, who was in my class, absolutely couldn't believe that I'd won the boxing match. He's the only person I knew who had two sets of boxing gloves, and for the next week or two we periodically boxed each other after school. I pounded him every time, so he started proclaiming my virtues as a boxer, and within a couple of weeks, life got back to normal for everybody with the exception of the kid who used to be my friend.

Square dancing was an activity that was in vogue at this time just about everywhere. My parents and the parents of many of my friends would spend a night or two each week, learning and performing dances to the commands such as: "allemande left or right, dosado, ladies in – men sashay, all eight circulate," etc. from a square dance caller. One of my teachers volunteered to teach students interested in learning square dancing to come to school at 7:00 A.M. The group was called "The Early Birds," and eventually performed at an assembly. I enjoyed the activity and discovered it was a good way to meet girls.

I also took ballroom dance lessons during the school year.

(From *An Island In Time II: Coming of age in the 1950's*) *"Fortunately, I wasn't the Lone Ranger in this endeavor. Several of my 8th grade male friends also wrangled with their mothers about an activity that sounded about appealing as being drug through a cactus patch. Fridays, after school, we "whipped puppies" were loaded into a car and driven to the Women's University Club in downtown Seattle to spend an hour or so with many other 8th graders from all over the city. Just about everybody there, including the girls, had the same expression of utter amazement that so many mothers had hooked their kids into taking dance lessons.*

The lady who taught us must've worked on a cattle ranch, judging from the way she herded us around. The girl I got paired with was as mute as me; however, it's impossible to talk when you're holding your breath. We were directed in the box step and actually had to touch our dancing partner and move in unison. I felt like making a break for it, but noticed Mom was watching my every move like a cat observing a mouse, plus if I made it past her, there was a gauntlet of other mothers I'd have to get past. As I stumbled my way through the ever-repetitive movements, I noticed my partner had a face and blue eyes. I tried to fake a smile, but sensed that my lips might split, so tried to speak ventriloquist-style instead. The sound that emerged from my mouth momentarily scared both of us, but my awkward attempt to communicate came to an end when our dancing teacher announced: "You will now do the box step to music!" If we were water skiing it would be comparable to attempting to cross the wake for the first time. As the music started I "wiped out," but under the mothers' eyes I kept going, reasoning that if I could rub my stomach and pat my head at the same time, why not move my feet in a pattern to music? Before the end of the record I was able to get my eyes off my feet and actually glance at my partner to see that she had blonde hair and a nice looking right ear. When the music stopped we were commanded to clap, which I'm good at. Next, we were to introduce ourselves. I blurted out, in a higher than normal pitch, "Side step – I – I mean, my name's — (I searched my memory quickly but could only come up with a horse's name) Rex – I mean, Don. What's yours?" While she gained her "voice" – actually a whisper, I was able to see the unseen parts of her head and saw that she had a left ear, eyebrows, a nose and mouth. She realized, by the puzzled look on my face, that I wasn't able to hear what she said, so in a barely audible voice she repeated, "Cathy." I noticed she had braces, which actually didn't look all that bad. I didn't care if she had two heads and came from another planet because I had just talked to the first girl outside of my school, and we had learned how to dance!

After a couple of more weeks of pairing up at our lessons, we started talking to each other on the phone and I was able to develop some conversation skills, even though, at first, I had to write down a list of things to talk about. Eventually I worked up enough nerve to ask her if we could swap pictures, and finally to come to one of our neighborhood parties where we danced to our own records. Although we didn't communicate with each other after that, we both managed to develop our social skills with others outside our neighborhood circles."

Subjects taught by males attracted my attention. The shop teachers had quite a job on their hands with boys (girls took home economics) who liked to do unsafe things whenever the opportunity arose. Horror stories from the shop classes had to be relayed to me by those who were lucky enough to actually be at the scene, because although I signed up for wood shop or metal shop throughout the year, I got mechanical drawing.

My history class teacher was also the school's band and orchestra teacher. He also played the trumpet in a dance band. Like the trumpet player Louis Armstrong, Mr. Libby had played the instrument so much that his upper lip was permanently dented. When there were music assemblies in the 7th grade, it was evident that the music teacher knew how to produce competent musicians on various instruments. At the beginning of my 8th grade year, I signed up for beginning band as a trumpet player. I actually enjoyed playing my chosen instrument to the point of looking forward to practicing every night. The teacher thought I was good enough to be promoted to the more advanced band, but said I'd better stay with the beginners as a model to them. Now, that really encouraged me!

Me in 8th grade and 7th grade friend, Budd, a future restaurateur

~3~

High School

There was a family tradition to which I had looked forward: military high school. My father and two older brothers had graduated from Northwestern Military & Naval Academy in Lake Geneva, Wisconsin. I was totally psyched to attend this school, established in 1888, even though I would be away from my family and friends for months at a time. My brothers had spent a good deal of time prepping me for this adventure in education, and my peers seemed to be envious in a skeptical-kind of way.

My school home for four years

I became Cadet 77 (out of about 150). It took a while to adjust to a different way of life, such as wearing a uniform, pants with no front pockets, a tie, suspenders and shined shoes. I had to learn how to march with and without a 9 ½ pound M-1 rifle, do rifle exercises, know the meaning of bugle calls, clean my room, make my bed with hospital corners, help clean the wash hall (communal bathroom), live with a roommate, learn table manners, sing every morning in chapel, and generally use my time wisely.

The beginning of a school adventure, in uniform

Because the academy was billed as a college preparatory school, a college curriculum of subjects was required. Students had to take four years of English, three or four years of math, four years of science, two years of a foreign language, and other classes in social studies, history, etc. Besides the major subject requirements we had to take what were called minor subjects for four years: military science, religion and letter (to home) writing. My desire for male teachers was super-satisfied by the school's faculty, and I only had one female teacher during my tenure in this school. She was my English and speech teacher my senior year, and ended up influencing me to become a speech teacher 10 years later.

I became aware that many of my fellow cadets (military students) were not attending this school because they wanted to, and the inappropriate behavior some of them demonstrated had to be brought under control. Then there were smatterings of social misfits and borderline dunces.

One of the 'misfits', an upperclassman, was gifted in photography, spending his free time taking photographs or developing, printing and enlarging in the school's darkroom. I asked if he would show me how to work in the darkroom. I found it interesting and productive to experience how these photos would be included in the Academy's photojournalism publications. I also learned a great deal about cameras, lenses and composition from this student teacher. As a result of this activity, I took and taught several photography classes, even up to my 30th year of teaching.

Some students were in our student body as a safety precaution or a means of protection from "bad guys." I discovered some cadets' parentage were members of criminal-type mobs in the Chicago area. During my senior year a small-statured freshman would be visited by either his mother or father accompanied by two rough looking men. One time I observed one of the toughs accidentally expose a shoulder holster with a pistol under his jacket.

A kid in our school belonged to a Chicago gang of motorcycle riders who paid us a visit one Sunday. The school's Commandant of Cadets (an instructor), was on duty, so greeted the out-of-place intruders by admiring their motorcycles and demonstrated his riding skill by buzzing off on one of their bikes (with permission). When he returned, he explained why they needed to leave, which they did.

The aforementioned Commandant had a car that needed to have its three-speed transmission removed and replaced and asked a mechanically adept member of my class to do the job when he had the time. (This cadet later had a 40-year career as a heavy equipment mechanic) I knew next to nothing about mechanics, but thought it might come in handy someday, so asked if I could tag along to learn how to fix cars. I was trained in what tools to use and what different parts were called, then handed him tools and parts as he performed his skills. When the job was completed, it was discovered that the gears were upside-down, so where the reverse gear was, actually was the 3rd gear. The car's owner wasn't too happy, but the mistake was rectified and I got some good lessons to apply later in life. I had to replace a 4-speed transmission several years later, and was prepared for what I needed to do.

The headmaster (Superintendent), who was above everyone else in the chain of command, lived with his wife and family in a two-story apartment at one end of the school. He was a very imposing man with a rather calm demeanor, who dressed mostly in Episcopalian priest's garb except when the cadets marched on parade. Then he'd be in a military uniform with the rank of colonel. (Colonel Aide de Camp, Wisconsin National Guard).

His size gave off an aura that said, "I don't think you want to mess with me!" In my sophomore year, a certain disgruntled cadet (the 'mechanic') yelled an obscenity-laced tirade that echoed the full length of the school building as he made his way to leave the school (which was located out in the boonies). The headmaster was in the area of the door, and placed himself directly in front of the cadet and said, "Where do you think you're going?"

"I'm leaving this dump!"

The cadet was a pretty big guy, but our headmaster, who was a bit bigger, simply picked him up under his arms and turned him around, saying, "No you're not! Let's take a little walk to my office, OK?" The "little walk" resulted in that cadet graduating from the school three years later.

The only class the headmaster taught was Senior Religion. He knew his subject; however, he didn't know how to teach it very effectively. His delivery was in a bass-monotone which had a hypnotic effect on his audience. I'd try to get an understanding of his lectures and psych him out by engaging his eyes and nodding my head at the times I thought it appropriate. Because he saw me reacting to what he was saying, he assumed I could answer questions when he directed them at me. Unfortunately I had no idea what he was talking about. I wasn't the only one who had a problem with our instructor's hypnotic monotone, so some of us devised a plan to make him change the pitch in his voice by making distracting movements, coughing, clearing our throats, etc. When he'd had enough of our antics, he'd stop his lecture and chew us out, thus breaking the spell he cast over us.

Second in command was the school's principal, he also held the rank of colonel (Colonel GSC USAR) and dressed in the appropriate army uniform. He was a WWII veteran who had served in the Pacific Theater with stripes on his uniform showing 2 ½ years of battlefield experience. Rumor had it that he'd escaped from a tank that had been hit, and that it had left him shell-shocked which showed up as tremors in his hands. In my mind he was the epitome of what a principal should look like and how he should behave. His voice was one of authority and, if possible, to be avoided.

There was one event that I witnessed where a cadet got the better of the principal. Nobody would go into the principal's office without getting permission from the student Officer of the Day who had a table outside of the Colonel's office. One day after breakfast, when a cadet was refused by the school's nurse to issue him an excuse to miss class because of sickness, the spurned boy rushed up to the O.D.'s desk demanding to see the principal, but before the O.D. could say yeah or nay, the cadet barged into the office. The "voice" bellowed at the cadet to "Get out!" The cadet said, "I'm going to be sick!" The principal replied, "I don't care, get out!" The cadet threw up on the Colonel.

Corporal punishment in public school was generally dished out by the principal or his assistant or toady who wielded a large heavy paddle applied to the rear-end's of misbehaving students – so I've been told. Military school punishment had to be learned and was sometimes done before the fact, not by the faculty, but by a committee of seniors and aided by other upper classmen. It might be classified as group punishment for those who weren't up to par in their schoolwork and grades. Students received a grade report ever two weeks. Based on our grades in all our classes, teachers determined what grades we were capable of reaching or our "par" grade.

"All you miserable plebes squat at attention!" screamed the Battalion Commander. Thirty five of us quickly squatted on the study hall floor, looking like a group of Russian dancers poised to kick one leg, then the other in time to balalaika music. As our folded arms held away from our bodies started shaking with the strain of holding them up and our legs getting numb, our commander ordered the rest of the battalion who were starting to get raucous to hold their comments until we started "bouncing." "Plebes, you are about to learn a physical skill that you may have to use at various times this coming year." We squatters were instructed to leap forward and maintain the attention position with our arms and continue bouncing until we were told to halt. "Forward – Bounce!" The older boys shouted, laughed and whistled loudly as we made a miserable spectacle of ourselves. Our tormentors were veterans of military school hazing, and judging from their gleeful/angry facial expressions, they relished our predicament. The insane cacophony was deafening and my eardrums were actually crackling. 'This is a glimpse of hell' I thought when my legs rebelled and I collapsed in a heap. Hands of some of the older boys grabbed at my arms, pulling me to a squat, and I was forced to continue. Maybe this was the feeling one got when swept up in a lynch mob. When the agony was finally over for all of us initiates we had tears streaming down our faces, some were sobbing and, judging from the intense ringing in my ears, deaf. Through the ringing I discerned the voice of the Battalion Commander: "This is an example of what it will be like for you come grade reports and you get below a C-grade average. You are dismissed!" Very bad behavior brought about the school's version of hacking which was administered by a senior cadet officer with a swat with a sabre across the buttocks – something to be avoided.

We had our rooms inspected six days a week for cleanliness and neatness. Two or three of the military noncommissioned officers who were Regular Army sergeants, and the academy's Tactical Officer would use a five-point-rating system which ranged from a -2 to a +2. If the room scored in the negative range, the room's occupants were assigned to labor detail which might involve leaf raking, wood gathering, or other menial tasks after school. If the weather was unfavorable, the punishment involved marching with a rifle back and forth alongside the length of the school (350') for an hour or so after school.

"Major" Lilich was the school's tactical officer. "Major" L. was a serious-looking gentleman with a noticeable foreign accent. He wore an army-type uniform, but with the insignias and badges of our school. Supposedly he had been in the Serbian Army during WWII, and allegedly was a 1939 European tennis champion. He fled the communist Tito occupation of Yugoslavia after the war, and somehow ended up at our school along with some of his countrymen who worked in the school's dining room and kitchen. "Maj," as we called him, demanded our best effort in everything we did, whether in our appearance or responsibility to duties we had as cadets. As the school's tennis coach he kept a close watch both on and off the court on his players' performance. He kept all of us in line.

The position of P.M.S & T (Professor of Military Science & Training) was led by a Regular Army major, who was in charge of a staff of two master sergeants and a sergeant first class. These soldiers taught military-related classes and saw to our training in order to keep us accredited as Reserve Officer Training Corps (ROTC) certified. If we went to a college that offered ROTC training, our first two years of training would be satisfied.

All the army instructors did a thorough job of teaching us in things military to the point that I found four years after graduation, when I enlisted in the Army, I was heads and shoulders ahead of most of the other recruits and could teach my platoon everything they needed to know, and was designated "Distinguished Trainee."

The sergeant first class instructor was especially memorable in his ability to instruct. His demeanor was perfectly military and he was interesting and entertaining. He had combat experience in WWII and the Korean War as a rifleman, meaning he was a foxhole soldier who because of his savvy, survived over three years of combat. As an instructor/coach of the school's rifle team he produced a group of sharp shooters who won first place in Wisconsin rifle team competition. He also put together a National Rifle Association Club, in which I participated and earned every possible medal. When I was in army basic training, I put my learning to the test and earned marksmanship medals using two different rifles.

I struggled with mathematics for three years, but because our teacher persisted and gave us individual instruction, I had an understanding of how to use a slide rule (before calculators) and how to use math tables which allowed me to be able to function in my technical job in the Army and as a wholesale grocery & produce salesman (figuring profit for pricing). This teacher was the first person to suggest that I would be a good teacher.

The most interesting teacher I had taught chemistry. He really knew his subject, but because of his lack of instructing, class management skills and my rote memory disability, I managed to flunk first year Chemistry in college.

I took notes primarily on his inability to pronounce his Rs and Ls. His opening statement was, Good moaning (morning) fewwows (fellows), my name is --- (unfortunately, his first and last name had Rs in them) and this is chemistwy (chemistry)." We thought he was joking, so burst into laughter, only to find out when we looked at some of the "chemicos" (chemicals) on the "pewiodico chawt" (Periodical Chart) that H stood for "hydwogen, Li stood for "Withium", Al stood for "Awuminum - he actually talked that way!

On lab day he displayed his lack of understanding of mischievous boys who regularly, fouled up procedures which led to an explosion or two, and couldn't figure out why his white lab coat had colored ink stains & holes. The pranksters took advantage of his naivety and would walk up behind him with a liquid ink pen and shake it like a fever thermometer, spraying permanent ink on his white coat. The holes were caused by glass eye droppers full of hydrochloric acid. The acid was also dripped onto his shoes, and sometimes we could observe our teacher walking around with his shoes smoking. Primarily, there were only two students giving him a rough time, but when others saw weaknesses, they would sometimes join in on the antics.

The troublemakers did do a dangerous thing that finally caused them to back off. The experiment on lab day came with a warning to us to be extra careful in following instructions. We were to GENTLY heat the test tube until the chemicals changed colors. The two lab gremlins deliberately didn't follow the "gently" part, and the one holding the test tube had it explode, leaving him with a black face and empty test tube holder. Miraculously, none of the shattered glass caused any injury.

One teacher who impressed me with his versatility and knowledge of a variety of subjects, skill as a coach, and passion for teaching, was a gentleman of slight stature, good nature, and had a way with words. He taught American history, economics, sociology and religion, plus he coached the debate and golf teams. His sociology class was so interesting, that I considered majoring in it in college.

My only female teacher, who taught English and speech, proved to be a life-influencing teacher. Her pleasant-but-firm instruction caused me to find my voice, so to speak. Up until I was in her class I was very reluctant to volunteer or ask questions. She opened my eyes and understanding of how to organize and present topics orally. I discovered that I had a latent ability that would prove to be extremely valuable for the rest of my life.

The minor subject of letter writing, which were weekly letters home that were corrected and graded, helped me in composing. The corrections in grammar, punctuation and spelling pointed out weaknesses I could overcome by learning from mistakes. After four years, I was really good in writing compositions.

The academy didn't have a traditional marching band, but rather an impressive drum and bagpipe group called field music. Those who played musical instruments other than drums and bagpipes, met once a week under the direction of a music teacher from outside of our school. I wanted to continue playing trumpet, so joined the group. After we had mastered one tune, we worked on learning another, but had a lot of trouble, because a fellow trumpeter would continually goof up in one spot. Supposedly, we were to learn three songs to play for a school performance. The headmaster happened to visit our practice session where we bogged down, and said that we needed to work harder if we were going to perform for an audience. Our director, feeling the heat, urged us to make a supreme effort on our playing. Unfortunately, in several more attempts, the rogue trumpet player purposely goofed up every time. The director, finally reaching the end of his patience, threw an uncontrolled fit by snapping his baton, throwing music stands and storming out of the school. As we sat at our chairs in embarrassed conversation, a cadet came into our practice area and told us he had seen the director drive off in his car. The cadet also said he had siphoned gas out of the director's car. We never saw that music director again, and because one guy didn't try to improve, we never again got a band organized. The troublemaker didn't stay at the Academy long enough to graduate.

After our music group disbanded, I was approached by the school's bugler to find out if I wanted to help out in blowing bugle calls. I thought it would be an opportunity to keep up my lip-strength in case another band might start up. It ended up that I eventually became a bugler for three years, and I never had an opportunity to use my trumpet again.

All the other teachers I had throughout high school were competent in their teaching and prepared us for college entrance.

We live in a world in which most of us aspire to be superior, but are foiled by our own limitations. ~ B. Prelutsky

"All animals are created equal, but some are more equal than others." *~ George Orwell*

Almost everyone enjoys recognition and praise and likes to show off, but only the top performers receive special recognition - many times without really trying. I thought back to those like Tommy, in first grade, and the three-year-old genius brother of "snake boy."

Because students at the academy wore exactly the same uniform, we were only different by rank chevrons, ribbons, medals, pins or merit chords attached to our dress uniforms. Seniors who had received varsity letters could wear white letter sweaters on Friday. Student body leaders were awarded sabers which were worn on Parade Day. At the end of each semester students who were academically in the top 10% of their class received a small silver star to be pinned onto their dress uniform. This little star distinguished the academically gifted from the rest of us - Orwell's "more equal than others."

Try as I might, I had great difficulty performing in anything involving rote memory of anything more than a few items. I would have to repeat information over and over until it stuck with me, like the Lord's Prayer or Pledge of Allegiance. When I was in Boy Scouts, I didn't earn my First Class Badge because of Morse code. Memorizing words to poems, bible verses or music were often beyond my memorization capability; however, musical tunes I got right off the bat, like bugle calls - remembering words was a different matter. There was a radio program called *"Name That Tune"* where contestants tried to guess a tune with the fewest number of musical notes. I was very good at recognizing tunes, and would have been a great contestant. It was obvious to me that though I might not be outstanding in academics or athletics, I was still able to function at an above average level. I figured that other students and athletes must be in the same boat, or in Orwell's "all animals are equal" group. My life philosophy became "Do the best you can with what you've got." Winston Churchill's mantra: "Never, never, never give up!" was a close second.

Athletics was not my cup of tea, although I did turn out for tennis and football and proved to be mediocre. My roommate, however, excelled in every sport he participated – reinforcing in my understanding of life, that some cats got it, and some cats don't. I enjoyed watching all competitions, so I was encouraged to be assistant manager, then manager for basketball. I learned how to take care of the team's equipment, keep the locker room in order, and run the clock and be a score keeper; valuable skills in responsibility. As a bonus, I was able to travel with the team in the school's Cadillac limousines, which made a big impression wherever we went.

Head coach aka "Tuna Ben" S. was the antithesis of the coach in my junior high school. He had the ability to encourage and get the most out of any student who truly wanted to try out for practically any sport, and managed to schedule athletic competitions with schools in neighboring states. We even competed with the Wisconsin School for the Deaf in football and basketball which made me realize that even though students may have a handicap, they can learn how to deal with it and can perform very well in the same arena with those who don't have handicaps. I was always impressed and freaked-out by the fact that their school had cheerleaders. Their cheers sent a shiver up our spines because of the way they were delivered. It reminded one of how zombies might deliver them – monotone. The football players' only sounds were grunts and squeals when tackled. The quarterback gave hand signals instead of voice commands. It was like they operated through ESP!

After my freshman year the school's hazing of cadets gradually subsided, but there was a cadet in my class who was hazed fairly regularly throughout his first three years and survived. His mistreatment reminded me of 5th grade when we drove a kid to go nuts and drop out of school. In this case the cadet seemed to run a three-year gauntlet of harassment, yet I don't recall any faculty member coming to his defense. I only recall one time when a faculty member gave him a compliment. On a very cold Sunday after the battalion (student body) marched in a parade, the PMS&T chewed out everyone for the sloppiness in our marching posture (sort of hunched up because of the temperature). He said only one cadet appeared to stand tall and look like a true military cadet – the school runt! Of course this simply served to anger those who picked on him. Their attitude was, "The audacity of this runt!" This boy stayed about the same size from his freshman year to the beginning of his senior year. He had a higher than average voice pitch and seemed to use precise pronunciation of his words. He also had an annoying personality which projected a "kick me" feeling to those he interacted with.

At the beginning of 11th grade

At the beginning of my senior year, I heard him squealing in rage at someone in his room, "I'm going to kill you!" and when I came up behind him he had a plebe cornered while he held a golf club poised for action. I grabbed his arm to prevent him from whacking his adversary, and my hand completely encircled his arm where his bicep was. I dismissed the plebe and sat down with the school's runt to find out why this altercation occurred. It seems the picked-on senior had had enough hazing, and the plebe thought he could get away with picking on someone smaller than himself. I felt that a senior cadet, no matter his size, should get respect from a plebe and from all those younger than him – and even his fellow seniors. He then asked me, "Why does everyone pick on me?" I didn't beat around the bush and told him, with the emphasis on his size. The fact that my hand had completely encircled his bicep, made me realize that this poor kid had arms about the size of an infant and probably had barely enough strength to lift his rifle. He asked me what he might do for his situation, and I suggested getting hormone shots. I don't know where that idea came from, but he got his parents' permission and got the shots. They made a transformation of the cadet, and he gained height, weight, a lower voice pitch, pimples, and whiskers. At the end of the year, he gave me gifts of a key fob and a conch shell, to thank me for encouraging him. He told me, "You are the only person in this school that is my friend."

Attending a military school involves a hefty price tag, so when a cadet is kicked out, there needs to be a very good reason. Those kicked out during my four years were for: theft, burglary (of summer mansions nearby), continual fighting/threatening, attempted suicide, threatening with a weapon and, accosting a teacher. Also, there were some cadets who were asked not to return because of lack of academic progress.

~4~

College

Academically, I believed I was prepared for college. Upon admission to the University of Washington I was able to take the classes needed in order to pursue a course of study in pre-dentistry. I had told everyone who inquired as to what I wanted to be when I grew up, that I wanted to follow in my father's and grandfather's footsteps as a dentist. Since I'd done fairly well in high school, I thought it wouldn't be all that difficult in college. I held this point of view until I got my first quarter's grades. I got Cs in everything except P.E. (volleyball) where I got a B and chemistry an E. I was placed on probation for low scholarship right off the bat! Reality took hold, and I realized I wasn't going to be a dentist. I changed my major to Pre Major, meaning I was still in the College of Arts & Science but didn't have a clue as to what I might do.

Some of my freshman classes had over 100 students, and the teachers weren't all that engaging or particularly interested in student achievement. Their lectures were more like showing how smart they were, like in the chemistry class when the instructor wrote as fast as he could, erasing the blackboard immediately, and would repeat the process while barely move his feet.

I was particularly vexed by my sociology class where the teacher allowed those who smoked to do it, if they brought an ashtray. Those in the rear of the classroom could only partially view the blackboard and teacher through a thick cloud of noxious smoke. Cigarette company representatives handed out sample packages of five cigarettes to students who wanted them as we walked onto campus. Evidently, most of us in the sociology class took the samples and smoked all five cigarettes during the hour of class. I recall a question on our final exam asking us to list the steps in order to smoke marijuana. This was in the days where in most cities it was very unlikely one could find drug dealers, and virtually no body considered smoking pot. Whereas my high school sociology class made the subject matter interesting, and controlled the class - the college teacher just didn't cut it.

My second quarter proved to be much better and I had much better success with all my classes except math. I had full professors for all but one subject and received three Bs, a C and an E in Trigonometry. The Trig. Prof. was very good, but I had a strenuous P.E. class (weight training) before the math class, and about half-way through the class I would fall asleep. This was the only class that I ever fell asleep in from grade school through college. I opted to take this class again over summer quarter, and much to my regret, got an unqualified teacher who was a certified midget, with a squeaky voice, spoke with a thick foreign accent and regularly made errors in his calculations. I managed to get a C.

A class I took in psychology peaked my interest and the professor used experiments with our class as participants. This was the first college class where I didn't feel letdown as a student.

After enrolling in a class titled Classics (Latin & Greek Current Usage) I was told by a fraternity brother, who was a junior, that I had made a big mistake. It seems he had to take that class three times just to get a C. Actually this class helped me to better understand English, and I was glad I took it.

Third quarter found me taking another psychology class and sociology class. The reason for taking the psychology class was because my first exposure was so interesting. However, the professor of this psychology class proved to be a strange duck and had a very distracting habit of licking his moustache so frequently that several of us in the class would keep count of how many times he licked in an hour, and compare counts of licks-per-hour (LPH). The sociology class, I thought, just had to be better than the first one I took, but other than lack of cigarette smoke, it wasn't. Scratch further sociology classes.

So – the summary of my first year of college pointed out my obvious weaknesses of subjects I shouldn't be taking: Subjects that rely on rote memory and mathematics. I decided to change my major to Business.

Coming to a large university and joining a social fraternity wasn't a good recipe for a socially-deprived student like me. The four years spent in military school hadn't exactly readied me for unhindered exposure to the fairer sex. There was a lot of catching up to do at the expense of my scholarship. Freshmen desiring to join the members of Greek social fraternities/sororities had to go through training and instruction into the particular social structure of the particular group that has accepted them as pledges. It's like being on probation for a year, and if you are able to qualify academically, fit in socially, and jump through the hoops, you become a bonafide card-carrying member.

My fraternity pledge class - 1957

According to the *fraternityadvisor.com*, the main reasons Why Guys Join a Fraternity are: 1. Looking for acceptance – looking for a place to fit in; 2. To get a job – a resume builder; 3. Leadership experience (house manager, house president, etc.); 4. Their friends are joining. I would add 5. To meet sorority girls.

Throughout the year we initiates were required to learn the Greek alphabet, our fraternity's history, and songs on which we would be quizzed or demonstrate every week. We also had to perform "house duties" such as cleaning every Saturday, and go as a group to home football games. A senior fraternity brother was assigned to each freshman as a 'big brother' who knows the ropes, guiding his fledgling 'brother' in scholarship and social activities. We also were encouraged to participate in the university's extracurricular programs like sports, politics, music, etc. There was precious little time to goof off or get bored.

My ability to sing with enthusiasm appealed to the upperclassman pledge trainer who appointed me to lead my pledge brothers in the singing of the fraternity's songs. During spring quarter all who were living in the fraternity house would visit sorority houses and serenade the fair young lassies with some of the songs we had learned. At this time there were two junior class Brothers that performed and sang solos. They wanted to form a quartet, so asked me if I could play a guitar. In 8th grade I'd taught myself how to play the ukulele and could play a mean version of "My Bonnie Lies Over the Ocean," but never learned how to play a six-stringed guitar. It so happened one of the duet had a four-stringed banjo tuned like my ukulele. Another of my pledge brothers who was a good singer and did play guitar was asked if he would like to perform in the quartet. We quickly learned a couple of songs to perform at our serenades, and gained some notoriety.

The Phi Psi Quartet – Ralph, Curt, Ron, Don

In the following year we got requests to sing at several venues on and off campus practically every weekend, and equally dumbfounding, we got paid to perform! We built up our repertoire to include popular and folk songs and could perform for at least a half-hour. Eventually the quartet performed our routine so many times it almost became boring. I had thought being "famous" would be an ultimate goal in life. But after performing for a group of hundreds of screaming girls in a theater-setting, and being asked for my autograph, I realized that professional entertainers, actors, et al. are just ordinary humans with an appealing talent. As far as I know, for next two years the quartet was the only paid performing singing group from the University. I remained amazed that I had been thrust into the limelight just because I had learned how to play a four-stringed instrument and could sing in key. During our performances I usually was the designated spokesman to introduce the songs, the members, and make small talk. I remember only one time when I got a little stage fright – when we had to wait for a star football player who was being honored at a banquet.

After two quarters of studying, socializing and bonding with my fraternity's 39 pledge brothers, only 18 survived to qualify to become members. Now came the initiation period called Hell Week, or the period (established in the 1850s) of building brotherhood by means of "ridicule, embarrassment, humiliation, social isolation, drills on nonsensical information, sleep deprivation, shower deprivation, degrading skits…" (*people.howstuffworks.com/fraternity*). We became suit wearing, smelly, mute zombies in order to become members of a Greek fraternal organization. Hell Week turned out to be a prelude to the harassment (only with important purposes) I would have to face for eight-weeks in Army Basic Training.

Social life became paramount over education during my sophomore year. Business administration classes didn't stimulate my interests, but a couple of professors did. One economics professor was a legend who really put himself into his lectures. I didn't study, watched rather than absorb what he was teaching – and failed the course. I repeated the course at night school with a professor who had three amazing abilities. He could speed read and remember everything he read. Those sceptics (I was one of them) put him to a test by giving him anything we wanted him to read, then return the reading material to be examined as he parroted to us what he read. In a matter of a few seconds this ability was demonstrated to be true. We had him repeat this feat using magazines, paperbacks and textbooks from other subjects. He explained to us how he didn't have to buy textbooks throughout college because he'd go to a University book store, find the books required for his classes and read and memorize them before attending his classes. Another skill he had was scoring at least 80% on <u>any</u> multiple choice test no matter the subject. He explained his methodology and gave us great examples which proved to be helpful when taking those kind of tests.

One of my pledge brothers got caught lying about what classes he was taking when he told one of our brothers he was taking a class at the same time from the same instructor the other brother was attending. The other brother said, "I've never seen you in the class." "Well, I've got my book right here," he explained, showing a book-covered book with the subject and number written on the outside (a standard practice to keep the book in good condition in order to resell the book for a higher price to a bookstore). The questioning Brother later checked the inside of the book to support his suspicion that another book was simply covered with writing on the cover of the class he wasn't taking. The suspicious student decided to follow the faker to campus to see what was going on, and found he would go to campus with a throng of other student, enter a building with others, but walk out another door and spend almost an hour in the Commons drinking coffee. Before the class hour was up he'd return to the building and join students coming out of class and return to the Commons. Evidently he was embarrassed to admit he had failed the course and was making it up at night.

A fraternity brother who was a class or two ahead of me would only come to the fraternity house to check his mail at the end of each month in order to pick up a check his parents sent him. He pulled off one of the most despicable scams I had heard of. He had quit going to school after his first two years, got married and worked at a job, without the knowledge of his parents.

Another married Brother worked for a soft drink company as a truck driver, and as a mobile vendor for the company at our University's home football games. One day when I returned to the fraternity house from a class, the soft drink truck was parked in front. Several freshmen were taking cases of pop from the truck and bringing them inside to place on large dining tables. Some were carefully removing the bottle caps and inspecting the bottoms for possible prizes of products or cash. The driver would then recap the duds with a bottle capper and place the recapped bottles in their cases to be returned to the truck. The net result of this deceptive practice netted the driver a cheapo camera worth about $5. Selling pop at football games resulted in the pop-man-scammer figuring out how to make personal monetary gain. He would buy used empty cups (mainly discarded cups) from people for 5-cents, rinse them out, and sell the pop from his dispenser at full price.

One of the reasons to join a fraternity is to find business connections. I found this to be true from my first year on and was able to get part-time jobs at a florist shop, electric razor shop, and as a milk truck washer for a large dairy. I always liked to learn how various businesses' operated, and I enjoyed working. My father's advice to me was, "No matter what job you have, do more than you have to."

I also experienced an active social life, which in the fraternity involved 16 parties we had to attend or be fined $5 for not attending. Over a four-year period I was never fined. I also spent minimal time studying for my classes, thinking that by simply attending classes and taking notes, by osmosis, I could pass. I completely flunked out of school after the second quarter of my sophomore year. In order to be reinstated, I needed to retake two of my failed classes. I also decided to take a class in speech. At the end of spring quarter I was reinstated, but put on academic probation. In other words, academics had to replace social life. It took two years for me to learn how to be a responsible student and to get serious about my life or face the consequences.

My third year found me once more changing my major. One subject that appealed to my curiosity was in Abnormal Psychology. The professor was an amazing lecturer who spoke nonstop each session of class. He also gave us subjects to choose to write about overnight, with the caveat that the paper had to be typed. To a nontypist this can be an overwhelming task, so I paid one of my fraternity brothers to type my paper. It was a disaster with so many typos I was graded down for sloppiness. This caused me to enroll in a business college where I took typing, shorthand and 10-key tabulator. The typing part of the class proved to be, and continues to be, one of the most beneficial abilities I possess. Although I am a slow, I am still able to plug along at a rate faster than I can write by hand.

I took a speech class at night from a teacher who had an odd way of encouraging and discouraging students. I worked hard at preparing and practicing my speeches, which I considered very good. There was an older gentleman in the class who not only didn't prepare, but would deliver under the influence of alcohol. Our instructor would praise his speeches to high heavens, leaving the man and the rest of our class dumbfounded. After the third speech, I decided to drop the class due to my frustration. When I informed the teacher of my decision he exclaimed, "Oh no, don't do that! Your speeches are outstanding. The reason for praising the drunk is to hopefully get him to put in more effort … but it obviously isn't working." Realizing that I enjoyed speech, led me to change from the College of Arts & Sciences (to the delight of the Dean) to the College of Communications. I enjoyed every class I took my senior year and considered becoming a disk jockey or radio or TV announcer right up until I got a letter from Uncle Sam advising me to report for a physical exam so I could be rated for a Draft Status.

~5~

From College to the U.S. Army

Heeding Socrates' philosophical proclamation: *"The unexamined life is not worth living,"* at age 21, I reflected upon my condition. I had spent four years scraping by in ever-changing majors at the University; lacking at least a year's worth of credit in anything. I was engaged to be married, with no prospects of permanent employment. I was virtually dependent on my parents for just about everything. Then, a notice from the Selective Service (Draft Board) informed me that I had to report for a physical exam in order to be classified for the Draft. Examining my pathetic state of being, I questioned the wisdom of Socrates, who would have failed as a motivational philosopher, just as I failed the 'worthwhile' exam.

I decided to report for a physical examination to be classified for my Draft status before the deadline of my 22nd birthday. Unable to fail the physical, I was classified 1-A, meaning I would be first in line to fight in a time of conflict. Alternative options were, I could join a Reserve unit and go through Boot Camp or Basic Training, followed by doing my duty in Active Reserve *one weekend a month plus two weeks of summer camp a year for six years*! – OR– I could go into the military for three years and not have any Active Reserve time.

I had spent four years living in a military high school guided by the call of a bugle. I dressed in a uniform, went through daily inspections, marched a million miles, could disassemble and reassemble an M-1 rifle, blindfolded, in about a minute and took Reserve Officers' Training Corps classes. The result of all that was I was steeped up to my eyeballs in militarism, so I wanted my military obligation over with as quickly as possible.

One of my R.O.T.C. instructors, a battle-scarred active duty army veteran (WWII & Korea) told us that he chose to be an infantry rifleman because he was good at it, but there were a lot of other options for "chickensh*ts," or those who didn't want to experience the pain and excitement of hand-to-hand combat. He showed us a bayonet scar suffered at Iwo Jima that was easily over 12-inches and explained: "I was using a flamethrower and advancing inland, when a Jap rose out of a foxhole and laid me open with a bayonet." (We had actually seen WWII battle footage and 'our sergeant,' with flame thrower, during the battle where the wound was inflicted. He claimed that only a minute later he had shed the flamethrower in favor of holding onto his intestines while looking for a medic.) I chose to be a "chikensh*t" after his war story. I figured *he* had too much testosterone mixed with a death wish. *I* didn't have a death wish.

Armed with my sergeant's insider information, I went to a Recruiting Office to check out my possibilities in the various branches of service. The Army had the least amount of time to serve to satisfy an enlistment obligation, with three years of active duty and no active reserve time. If I scored high enough in tests, I could go into the Army Security Agency which NEVER went into combat. A high score would also qualify me for Officers' Training School, allowing me to get higher pay—extending my enlistment time.

I got good scores, there weren't any major military conflicts anywhere in the world, so joined, much to my fiancé's consternation, as a 'grunt soldier' for three years.

Basic Training

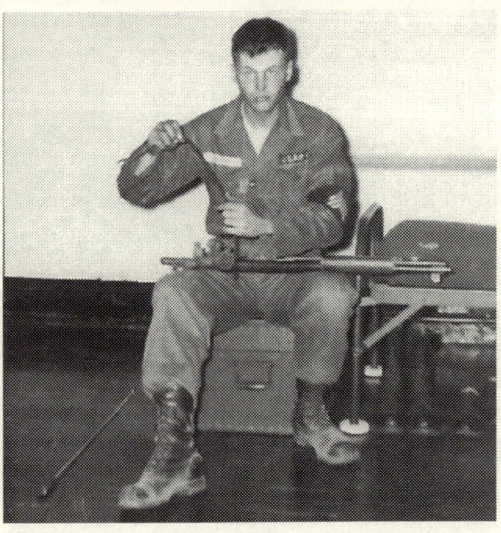

At the end of a day of training

I did my eight weeks of Basic Training at Ft. Ord, California, which was mainly an intense repeat of my high school training. Military school training proved to be valuable, and after demonstrating my military abilities I became a platoon guide. I wore an arm band with sergeant stripes and was placed in charge of 60 guys who I had to teach the fundamentals of just about everything, like marching, close order drill, making beds, cleaning rifles, shining shoes/boots, etc. One benefit to my position was that I had my own room. But just as my job of bugler in high school, I was the first one up in the morning and last one to bed at night. Also, the assigned job of mail clerk gave me the responsibility of handing out mail. This allowed me to associate all those names with the faces of the guys in my platoon.

My Basic Training Platoon – I'm front center

Just about every bit of military jargon, military technique, rule, nomenclature, etc. became second nature to every trainee by the end of our eight-week introduction to the U.S. Army. The last week of Basic, our Senior Drill Instructor gave a pitch for making the Army a career. (Like I wanted to spend 20 years of my life with the likes of him?) At one point he asked the rhetorical question, "Where else can you get a month's paid vacation to start?" An anonymous voice responded, "Teachers get <u>three</u> months." *A seed was planted.*

Also, near the end of Basic, one of our training officers asked if any of us could type and might want to fill a spot as a company clerk. I volunteered, interviewed for the position, and was to report to the job at the end of my training. A day or two later I was notified that that position was no longer available because the guy who had that job decided to reenlist for his position. The officer who had interviewed me felt that he had let me down so offered to get me into any school associated with the Army Security Agency for which I was qualified. I was fed up with going to school, and asked what the shortest-length course might be.

Advanced Training

I was sent to Fort Devens, Massachusetts for five-months. I had to learn how to type on what is called a 'mill' (only upper-case letters and numbers). At the beginning of each session we were asked whether the musical beat to which we typed should be ragtime jazz or classical. One day we marched to class during a hurricane. We were soaked, and peeled off all our clothes except our skivvies. That session we typed to jazz.

While we were waiting for our security clearances to come through, we were taught the fundamentals of what we would be doing at our final duty stations. There were mathematical principles involved along radio bearings which were sent by code over various distances – which didn't give us any idea of what we would actually be doing. We were told that we were involved with radio intelligence and our job title was Direction Finding Plotter Analyst. Chances were, according to rumors, that we would be sent overseas to Turkey or Korea. We took this rumor with a block of salt because if we hadn't heard a rumor by noon, we'd start one. By December, we all received our clearances, and could pick where we wanted to go, according to our ranking of scores on various tests during our training. The assignments were in Japan, Germany, Korea and Viet Nam (not yet declared a war zone). I got northern Japan and was slated to ship overseas in January of 1962.

Shipping Overseas on a Troopship

What I learned on the troopship, *USS General Breckinridge,* was; it was not built for comfort ex., rows of narrow bunks stacked four high with another row of bunks directly next to yours; there's nothing to see at sea except, if you were lucky enough to have job allowing you to have access to the fantail, then you were able to watch the daily weather balloons launch; working in the galley isn't a great way to spend your days, especially on rough sea days when full garbage cans had to be taken two flights up ladder-like stairs to be dumped into the ocean at the stern of the ship (before EPA regulations); we could get to our lifeboat stations very fast, even in rough seas, after several attempts; at sea, cigarettes are 11-cents a pack, so it was the beginning of developing a lung-destroying habit for many troops; anybody might be picked to be the ship's barber, and every head must be shorn before the end of our 13-day Pacific Ocean cruise. All of the troops who survived the rough journey learned to adjust to the ship's rolling, lurching and crashing into the surf and developed 'sea legs.' When we disembarked the ship and lined up in formation it was difficult to keep from weaving- that is, until we experienced an earthquake!

~6~

Overseas

I finally arrived at what was to be my home for 26-months, the 12th USASA Field Station located at Chitose, Hokkaido, Japan. As we newbies came onto our base by bus, we drove past an unoccupied three-story concrete building. A sign on it read, *Kuma Station – Hibachi Hall – Test Center Laboratory Housing – 768 Brave Men – We accepted it – Tho we don't understand it.* It seemed the cement structure that was meant to be our barracks didn't have a required heating system needed in the very frigid winter temperatures of the northern Japanese island, meaning we had to be billeted in Quonset Huts built soon after WWII.

My home in 1962

We troops were assigned to, what were called *'Tricks'* (work groups living together in the Quonsets) which worked in rotating shifts – Days, Swings, Mids. These shifts were for six days on with two days off. After two days off, the tricks would change shifts, work six on, two off, change shift, etc. This work schedule could seriously mess with one's mental time clock, and the strain drove some guys to drink way more seriously in order to cope with the mind-numbing schedule. I don't know of many sober guys who really got the hang of it. Fortunately, I managed to get assigned to a permanent day shift. Several guys I worked and lived with became functional alcoholics who influenced my decision to not follow in their dysfunctional footsteps.

My residence for 1962

Soon after starting my job, I was told of a week-long snow & ice festival in the large nearby city of Sapporo. Using the information supplied to me by my working companions, I learned how to travel by bus and how to read Japanese signs of what I needed to know. It reminded me of when I took the bus to downtown Seattle when I was in second grade. Because of the festival, the bus was jammed and I spent the entire hour-long ride standing.

Downtown Sapporo, Japan

I'm about 5'10", but seemed to be a head taller than most Japanese. When I got off the bus, I looked around the throngs of people to see if there were any Americans I could talk to. There wasn't another white person to be seen in the thousands of people in attendance, so I got busy looking at the giant ice and snow sculptures covering several blocks in the city.

Sapporo Snow Festival

Within 45 minutes of arriving at the festival, a black-uniformed male stopped in front of me and started a conversation in English that would change the course of my life. "Excuse me," said the uniformed boy/man, "may I speak with you in English?" Extending his hand, he continued, "My name is Kadzuo Yamamoto, or Yama. Would you let me buy you a cup of coffee and practice my English with you?" As it appeared he was sincere and I was becoming cold, I accepted his invitation. Making our way through the crowd, Yama took me about three blocks to the Sapporo Grand Hotel, the only Western-style hotel in the city. The ground-floor of the hotel had a crowded restaurant where we managed to get a table for two. I discovered my coffee companion was only a year younger than me, and was a medical student at the nearby Hokudai University (University of Hokkaido). There were several students in his medical classes that were interested in practicing their English conversation skills and Yama was a sort of recruiter for his classmates to find an American to practice with. "Would you be interested in meeting with us next week? We will pay for your bus fare." Geez, how easy would that be? I agreed to meet him at the bus terminal and meet with his friends. A week later, I was met at the Sapporo Bus Depot by Yama and another student named Nishi Yakamori. We caught a streetcar to Hokudai and walked to the medical school's well-worn wooden building and to a lecture classroom. I was greeted by over 40, mostly male, uniformed-students who applauded as I walked into the room. Strangely, I wasn't overwhelmed by the experience and treated it like a dream. As Yama introduced me, I asked myself, 'Is this experience really happening?' Similar to today's Press Conferences, each student introduced themselves and proceeded to ask a question. I remember two of the questions: "Do you have lots of Indians in the United states?" and "Is it true that Americans don't take baths?" Some of the questioners weren't very proficient in their English, so Yama or Nishi acted as translators. After the Q&A session, I was treated to a meal and a couple of beers at a beer hall, and given remuneration for bus fare. I also was invited to come back the next week, if I wanted to. Primed with such an exhilarating experience, I agreed.

The next week's get-together attracted a few more curious students who asked more questions. After they had drained my brain, Yama thanked me and asked the gathering if they would like to continue our English meetings, only with the purpose of learning spoken American English and being able to understand and speak it well enough to possibly become interns in American military hospitals. About half of the group raised their hands. Then I was asked if I would agree to become their teacher? In exchange, they would pay my expenses and teach me about their culture.

Yama, Nishi and I spent quite a bit of time brainstorming ideas of how to run the class. Besides vocabulary, they wanted colloquialisms and common expressions they might encounter in medical settings. And, would I type up the lessons so everybody in the class could have a copy? I started feeling panicky, but reasoned this would give me inroads to Japanese society that most other Americans would never have – and I would be able to improve my typing.

At first, virtually all of my off duty time was spent typing lessons four at a time by using carbon paper. Forty copies accompanied me to the next meeting at the university's lecture hall. About 35 students plus a university medical professor greeted me, and *I became a teacher* ('sensei' in Japanese). The class decided to call our assembly the Ducks' Club, because my first name, Donald, was associated with Donald Duck.

Future M.D.s forming the Ducks Club

From that first encounter a group of about 20 future doctors met with me every week for about a year and then about 10-15 who continued with me until my military service tour was completed. The classes were held in a lecture room at the University of Hokkaido, with post-meetings at a beer hall or coffee house. This wonderful experience took root in my mind, and I resolved that upon returning to civilian life, I would complete my education and become a teacher.

Ducks on a field trip to Dr. Kodama's Ainu Museum

Besides the Ducks, another group of university students, studying to be medical researchers, asked me to teach them for a year. One of their professors, a medical doctor, paid me to make editorial, English grammar and punctuation corrections on a manuscript for a book he was having published.

Our military post commander received a request from a city manager or mayor of the southern port city of Hakodate asking if it would it be possible for a soldier who was teaching English to be sent to their city to teach English phrases, pronunciation, etc. to various schools, businesses and institutions. A call went out to the few of us who performed such classes off Post to report to the commander and state our qualifications in order to do Temporary Duty (TDY) for this mission. I was a shoe-in because of my experience and also because I had a slide-show of the 1962 Seattle World's Fair – my home city.

All my expenses were paid, and I spent a week teaching in all levels
of schools (where I also made several hours of audio tapes), English
Speaking Societies, department stores, and even a hospital. I also met a
Trappist monk (the ones that take a vow of silence) who was the only one
who could negotiate with those on the outside-world. It just so happened
that this monk was the only one of his order who was Caucasian, and he
spoke a form of English called "Brooklynese" i.e. he was from Brooklyn.
Fortunately, I had a roommate on post that was from Brooklyn, so
understanding him was easy. All of these experiences solidified my
desire to return to college and become a teacher.

Teaching ladies at an English Speaking Society gathering

~7~

Return to Civilian Life

Back in the States, with the intention of seeking a degree in education, I went to the University of Washington to register for the spring quarter. Upon my arrival, I was greeted by a crowd of Viet Nam/Draft protesters that were disrupting the education process. So much for returning to college at this time.

Meanwhile, I needed to be able to support myself and would have to attend to the task of finding employment. I went to so many interviews I felt like I was a professional interviewee. I applied for unemployment compensation and found there was little encouragement in the offerings the State had to offer. However, I applied for a job in a shoe store displaying a sign in its window advertising "Help Wanted." After an interesting week, I had learned the psychology of selling shoes. If a pair of shoes in a certain style or color didn't fit, there was a shoe stretcher that might help. But if it didn't, you could disappear from view and do nothing to the shoe, and tell the customer to, "Try it now." Nine out of ten times the shoe would fit.

Salesman

At the end of a week at the shoe store, I received a call-back from one of my interviews informing me that I had a job. I was totally surprised, because it was to be a job as a wholesale grocery and produce salesman. I had virtually no knowledge of this industry, but this turned out to be why I got the job. The company wanted to train (indoctrinate) a couple of us with no experience in grocery stores or fruit stands to be indoctrinated in their company's brands and products.

The training began in the large produce warehouse with on the job training where we were exposed to and performed virtually every job in the facility. We unloaded boxcars; sorted, sized and packaged potatoes and tomatoes; placed stalks of bananas in ripening rooms; made salads for restaurants and institutions; loaded the trucks for their routes and unloaded them at their destinations.

We were taught about fruits and produce I didn't know existed, and how they were sold by size, quantity or weight. Every product was introduced in person, and many times tasted, so when we tried to sell something less familiar to the customer we knew what we were talking about.

The company's five-story dry goods warehouse contained canned fruits & vegetables, sugar, flour and spices. Each of these items were in different sized containers or packages and also different qualities ex., larger size beans or peas are considered second-best. Periodically the salesmen would have what were called "cuttings" where different brands of canned fruit or vegetables would be examined and tasted in order to know what brands were of what quality.

After a month or so of training, we were sent out with salesmen to learn techniques used for different types of customers, like stores, restaurants, institutions. Eventually, we wrote and priced, then organized the orders in which they would be loaded and unloaded from the delivery truck. The company had warehouse facilities all over the state, so we were sent to other sales territories in order to learn how different, more rural locations operated.

To complete my training and familiarize me with the ins and outs of the fruit, produce and grocery business, I was sent to a smaller facility located in Bellingham, near the Canadian border. I shadowed a salesman for about a week in order to learn a territory and how to write orders. I had been there only a week when the salesman quit his job with the company in order to start his own produce business, turning over his company territory to me. I ended up working the territory for another two or three weeks, until a veteran salesman could be sent to relieve me.

Back in Seattle, I was put to work in the company's large multi-storied grocery warehouse which was in the midst of filling orders for fishing boats headed to Alaska. After a frenetic week of filling orders, I received my first and life-changing assignment to Wenatchee in Central Washington. A salesman (one of three) had been let go because of shady dealings, and his territory was running down because of competing produce and grocery companies. My job was to rebuild the territory.

My Company Car

My arrival coincided with a company-sponsored dinner and dance at the local Elk's Club. Because I knew nobody in the area, one of the salesmen managed to fix me up with a girl he knew who had recently returned to Wenatchee to work as a secretary for the Wenatchee Valley Junior College president. We hit it off! (Eleven months later, while I was in Everett, we became husband and wife.)

Once I had rebuilt my territory, the Company sent me to the western side of the Cascade Mountains to the city of Everett, between Seattle and Bellingham. This territory was another territory that needed to be built-up. After two or three months I gave notice that I was going to quit and go back to school in order to become a teacher. My wife encouraged me to make this move, and volunteered to support us while I went to school.

~8~

Back to College

My wife, when we decided to have me go back to school, really impressed me with her abilities. When I decided to register for school, she went to Bates Technical College, and the Tacoma School District to apply for a job as a secretary. She had great references – one from her most recent job as Wenatchee Valley Junior College president's secretary, and her secretarial skills were also outstanding as she demonstrated that she could type extremely fast and take shorthand. She was offered jobs at both institutions and could begin in a matter of three days. She took the job at the Tacoma School District as secretary to the Director of Special Education, and would be making the meager sum of $300 per month! We weren't going to gain any weight on our food budget, but I had a few boxes of dented food cans missing their labels (most turned out to be hominy) to augment chicken backs and occasional cuts of meat priced under 35-cents a pound. We could pinch what pennies we had. Fish, clams, crabs and other seafood was available in front of our beach cabin, and I started growing a vegetable garden. We also never turned down invitations to dinners from family and friends.

We had saved up enough for one semester of tuition, and struggled to figure out how to pay for another three semesters, but by taking out a loan and receiving a partial scholarship for stagecraft (building sets, stage managing and all-around grunt) we got through my first year. My second year was paid for through the Veteran's Administration.

The University of Puget Sound (UPS) in Tacoma was only 15 miles from a small summer home on Fox Island my parents owned, and I had helped build, on Fox Island. I applied for admission to the education program with a major in speech and drama. Among the requirements was two years of foreign language. I objected to this requirement because I had taken two years of French in high school, and I couldn't see that a foreign language would help me in teaching. In order to waive the requirement I had to take a language proficiency test – which I failed – probably due to the fact that I hadn't used the language in nine years. When I got into the French class, everything I had learned in high school came back. I felt that I had spent good money to take a nonessential class. This experience prepared me for other frustrations I would face in the future for requirements of repeating classes I had already taken. Other than the foreign language frustration, most of the other classes I had to take were beneficial and the instructors were good.

One course I took in my undergraduate pursuit of teaching credentials was labeled 'the psychology of teaching,' but maybe a better name would have been 'teaching theories of the 19th century.' The teacher of the psychology class was a 'mental case' who went off the deep end and had to be replaced before the conclusion of the term. I'd entertained the idea of becoming a psychologist in my early college days, but after experiencing a number of 'strange' thinking and behaving professors, some with 'Dr.' before their name, I realized I wouldn't fit into their tribe/klatch/bunch, or whatever they call their compatriots. As President Reagan said, "It's not that they're ignorant. It's just that they know so much about what isn't so."

Fortunately, the class required some 'field study' and made visits to various grade levels and classes where teachers were observed in action. I went to daycare, elementary, junior and senior high schools, and a special education vocational school. After our observations we would discuss the classroom dynamics and ask questions.

The final project was to go to an institution for two weeks, pick a case study, and write it up. Through a lottery-type of assigning, I went to a daycare, which reminded me of visiting over-active puppies in a pet shop. I selected a four-year-old alpha male named Barry. I probably should give him the credit for selecting me. He introduced himself as, "My name's Bawy, but not Bawy Goldwato' (a politician at the time). It was interesting, but impractical for me who planned to teach high school. However, I was able to gain a bit of knowledge in crowd control.

When I reached the point where I did my student teaching I was placed in a large high school in Tacoma, not far from UPS. I was assigned to a drama class taught by a woman, and a speech class taught by a man. After a brief time of observation and explanation of material to be covered, I jumped right in. When my teachers were satisfied I could handle the classes, I finished out the duration of the semester and gave the students their grades. I felt confident that I could teach high school students. I was glad that the students I had been assigned to teach were, for the most part, the nonacademic types. I think they were surprised they actually learned and improved their skills when they applied themselves.

PART II

AS A PUBLIC SCHOOL TEACHER

~9~

Looking for a Teaching Job

With the end of my studies in sight, interviews for positions available in my specific subject areas of speech and drama were not readily available, but with an English minor, some school districts had openings in language arts.

It was never my intention to get a job 45 miles from my home. In a way, I took the job for spite. A job was offered to teach in a much closer school district, but a "sure thing" teaching the subjects of my major was dangled in front of me at the same time in the faraway district. The closer district said, "We'll hire you into a pool, to teach in the language arts area of junior and senior high schools." The sure thing job was teaching in the only high school – speech, drama, English and any other language art related subjects, plus I would coach debate & forensics and direct the plays. A contract would be ready for me to sign, but it had to be signed by the coming Friday. The closer job asked if I would sign a contract with them, also. I explained that another district wanted me to sign by Friday, so if they wanted me, I'd have to have a contract ready to sign by the same day, or I would go to the other district. I didn't get a response to the deadline until Monday when they said, "We have a contract ready for your signature." My response: "Sorry, I told you I had to know by last Friday. When you didn't respond, I drove to the other school and signed their contract."

It seemed like I drove for an eternity to get to the school where I would be teaching, and I had to stop in the small Norwegian fishing town of Poulsbo to ask directions. I had been asked by the assistant superintendent, who interviewed me at my college, to bring my wife because the high school's principal wanted to interview both of us before going to the administration office to speak to the superintendent. I thought the request a bit odd, but agreed, since I needed a job, and there weren't a whole lot of openings in any nearby schools for my subject areas of speech and drama.

The principal, a man in his late 50s, a seemingly pleasant person, asked my wife and me into his office. His 'interview' seemed more like a chat, and he wanted mostly to know about our marriage and compatibility. I later discovered my predecessor in speech & drama was leaving the district because he'd left his wife to marry one of his drama students, which caused some raised eyebrows in the community.

The school district's administration offices were located about three blocks away on the top of a hill which formerly housed a Nike Missile Site. An empty underground silo was steps away from the former HQ building and now the school administrations' building.

I entered the reception area, telling the receptionist/secretary I had an appointment. I was somewhat taken aback by the lady who had a cigarette in her mouth, and had a wheezy man's voice. After coughing for a spell, she informed me he'd be with me in a few minutes, "so sit down and wait." Because of her demeanor I wondered what I had gotten into, when the assistant superintendent, the one who had interviewed me, came out of his superior's office. When he spotted me, he smiled and said, "We've been waiting for you," and ushered me into the office.

The head administrator had been the district superintendent for several years and was approaching or was the age of retirement. He went over my teaching contract, explaining my duties, expectations and pay schedule. I had 30 hours beyond the required 180 credits required to teach, plus I had been told that I could start at the third year of experience because I had served three years in the army. I was also granted extracurricular pay for coaching debate and directing plays. The head man balked at the army experience counting for teaching experience, saying, "You can only get credit for the army years if it interrupted your college education and you were drafted. Do you qualify under either of these conditions?"

I smelled a skunk - called 'bait and switch.' I had been promised two years' experience for the three years in the service when I interviewed with the assistant superintendent, so objected. The difference in pay would be significant, plus every other district I had talked to, said that I would receive two years' experience credit. "Well, I'm sorry, but we can't give you credit," he said, "So you'll have to take it or leave it."

Looking at the assistant, I protested, saying, "You told me I'd get the service credit, didn't you!" Looking at his boss, he replied, "Yes. I told him he'd receive credit, sir."

"Well, our policy is only if someone is drafted out of college, will he receive credit for time served in military service."

I'd received my share of bullying and B.S. shelled out by my superiors in the army and other jobs I'd had, so called the Super's bluff. "Well, I've got a job guaranteed, including service credit that wants me to sign next week. No credit from you means I take the other contract."

"Go sit in the reception area, while I talk with my assistant," said the Super, "and we'll see if we can work out something."

Taking leave of their discussion, I walked to the waiting area where my beautiful pregnant wife was reading a well-worn *Mechanic's Illustrated* or other magazine. "They are trying to get out of paying service credit," I explained, "but they're talking it over, since it was promised me in the interview. If I don't get it, I'll sign with Tacoma."

I could hear the renegers having a spirited conversation[1], but felt fairly certain I'd get what I'd been promised. I knew that I was a rare commodity because schools having drama and debate couldn't just go out and find somebody like me. If I didn't get the job here, there were several districts closer to my home who wanted to snap me up to teach English or language arts subjects.

Within five minutes the Assistant came out and told me I had the contract the way I wanted it. When I walked back to the Super's office, he looked disgruntled. "We will include the experience credit; however, keep it to yourself[2]. Sign at the bottom of the contract and we'll expect you to report for duty at the high school two days before the start of classes. Welcome to our school district," he said as he extended his hand. I sensed he had to force a slight smile, but not enough to show his teeth.

---

[1] I found out later there were no other potential speech and drama interviewees.
[2] He'd pulled this bait and switch with other veterans. When the local Education Association got wind of it, he was censured and had to pay all veterans the service credit and apologize for his deceptive hiring techniques.

I examined the contract, noting the agreed-to credit was not there. In the recent past I had gone through an unpleasant time dealing with the Veteran's Administration and found that if I didn't have something in writing before I signed anything I'd go through months of rigmarole trying to get things straightened out. "Thank you for honoring our original agreement; however, I would like the contract retyped with the change before I sign. If it's not convenient, I could come back on Monday."

"Boy, you're pretty persistent, aren't you?" said the Super. I sure as hell hope you're worth all the trouble. I'll have my secretary retype it," he said as he brushed past me to the smoking lady. "Agnes, type this with the insertion of two years' experience on the pay scale." Placing her smoking cigarette in an already full ashtray, she went to a file cabinet, found a teaching contract and rolled it into her electric typewriter. I thought my wife was a fast typist, but this lady obviously had typed lots of contracts, and only moments later she had it completed and ready for my inspection. The cigarette in the ashtray had barely burned a quarter of an inch in the meantime. With all the jots and tittles taken care of, I signed.

My salary would be a little more than $6,000 per year – somewhat less than what I made as a produce and grocery salesman – which hardly seemed worth it, but I reasoned I could work my way up the ladder and perhaps make my way to the top of the pay scale ($13,000 with a PhD and 13 years teaching experience). At least I would make $200.00 more a month than my wife, a highly skilled woman, who was a secretary for the Director of Special Education in the Tacoma School District. She was scheduled to quit her job in October, just before her delivery date in November. We hoped to be able to put away enough money to pay the doctor before becoming parents. Even with my paycheck, our finances would be very tight. There was no leeway for any unexpected emergencies.

~10~

Let the Classes Begin!

My first year

Two days before I reported for duty as a bonafide teacher, all new teachers to the school district reported to a local church's basement for a welcome breakfast, where each of us was introduced to our fellow compatriots. *Eight* of us were new to the high school's staff.

I was to teach Drama, Speech and English 10. There were two business and typing teachers, a social studies teacher, a home economics teacher, a mechanical drawing teacher, and a Spanish/English teacher. Three of the eight had some teaching experience, but the rest were first-timers. I was suspicious about why so many of the total number of teachers were starting in 1967.

After the breakfast we reported to the high school to receive our teaching schedules and room assignments. Space in the 10-year-old building was at a premium. I moved every period to a different room or area, like the stage and the green room (dressing room for the stage). My office was one of the dressing rooms. I also taught a speech class among the stoves in the home economics room. For a six-period day, I was to teach five different classes, and I had no planning period. On top of this, I would have to direct the school plays and coach the debate and forensics teams. Other than the 25-minute lunch time, I had to run from one end of the school to the other. After the final bell rang, I corrected papers, planned the next day's classes, or went to teacher meetings. When all was said and done, I could go home. Many times I questioned my choice of occupations. Would I be able to keep my head above water, or would I be one of next year's departing members of the high school faculty?

Other Teachers' First Days

The beginning of each school year can be very stressful. New teachers – or for that matter, virtually ALL teachers are tested daily to see if they can hold up. I knew a girl who prepared to be an elementary school teacher, but didn't even last one day despite five years of classwork and an elementary teaching certificate.

Also, I taught with a teacher who on his first day of class in an old junior high school, got locked in the coat closet with no inside door knob, when a student slammed the door on him and wouldn't open it. After three class periods he was let out. With this humiliating experience behind him, he went on to teach for 30 more years.

First year's Classes, Activities & Supervision

My assigned classes filled every available desk or chair wherever I went in the painfully- overcrowded school building. Every classroom was full throughout the day, and even areas that were not intended for instruction, became teaching stations. My schedule showed that I had a speech class in the lunchroom *during* lunch. I ended up being moved to the home economics room that had the stoves. I realized now why the school had high teacher turnover – overcrowding – unrealistic expectations – low morale. However, I was a young army veteran, had gone through four years of military school, hell week in a college fraternity, worked six days a week as a salesman, six years of college and three years in the army under my belt – I thought I could withstand the challenges to come – and come - and come ……

Teaching Requirements and Salary

Lest the non-teacher reader think teachers have a pretty good deal with a whole bunch of free time after ONLY spending six hours a day on the job, I've got news for you. The school day may only be six hours (not counting a 25-minute lunch break), but then it's time to check homework, grade tests, prepare lessons for the next day's class for each subject or grade level taught, attend department meetings or faculty meetings, and supervise or coach activities or sports.

On top of all this, every faculty member was scheduled to supervise at so-many sporting events and after school dances. For a person like me, who lived so far away, it meant travel time and extra wear and tear and gas for my car. The dances were either with vinyl records or a live band. One live-band dance I chaperoned, the band was unable to perform even one complete tune. I don't know what they were thinking – maybe a miracle might occur and they would be able to play the tunes they had in their heads? We had to refund the attendees money, and the nervy band leader had the gall to ask to be paid!

Fifth Year Requirements

New teachers were required to take 15 credit hours of credit beyond the hours necessary to receive a B.A. degree within five years of beginning their career. Back in 1968 the advancement on the salary schedule enriched the teacher $178.50 or $14.875 a month.

1968-69

TEACHERS' SALARY SCHEDULE

BA	BA+15	BA+30	BA+45	BA+60	BA+75	BA+90
1st year	$5950.00	6128.50	6307.00	6545.00	6783.00	7021.00	7318.50
2nd year	6188.00	6366.50	6545.00	6783.00	7021.00	7259.00	7556.50
3rd year	6426.00	6604.50	6783.00	7021.00	7259.00	7497.00	7794.50
4th year	6664.00	6842.50	7021.00	7259.00	7497.00	7735.00	8032.50
5th year	6902.00	7080.50	7259.00	7497.00	7735.00	7973.00	8270.50
6th year	7140.00	7318.50	7497.00	7735.00	7973.00	8211.00	8508.50
7th year		7556.50	7735.00	7973.00	8270.50	8508.50	8806.00
8th year		7794.50	7973.00	8211.00	8568.00	8806.00	9103.50
9th year		7973.00	8151.50	8449.00	8806.00	9103.50	9401.00
10th year		8151.50	8330.00	8687.00	9044.00	9401.00	9698.50
11th year		8330.00	8508.50	8925.00	9282.00	9639.00	9996.00
12th year				9163.00	9520.00	9877.00	10293.50
13th year						10115.00	10591.00
Master	+357						

{Beginning Teachers holding a BA degree & Provisional Certificate will start at $6000.00}

My salary, when I began teaching in 1967, was at the BA+15 level of education, and to advance to BA+30 I only had to get another seven hours of credit. I took a two-hour class in early summer and a five-hour class toward the end of summer. I didn't have to pay to take the latter class because it involved spending nine days of living with emotionally disturbed children at a camp on a 13-acre island in Puget Sound, which had originally been used by pre20th Century Indians as a burial island. In 1946 the island was bought by a Tacoma physician who turned it into a boys' camp, named Camp TaHaDoWa. It just so-happened my home was across the water from the island and was only about 400+ yards away. I was assigned to eight 10-year-old boys and had a high school boy as my assistant. The boys under my care ranged in emotional disturbances as slight as gender identification issues to flat-out over-the-edge psychotic. The object of the camp, which was under the direction of the Pierce County Chief Psychiatric Social Worker, was to provide a near as possible normal camping experience for boys and girls from the ages six or seven to age 13, if they were not physically mature. Every night my assistant would keep watch over our cabin while we counselors would attend a meeting with the camp director and a psychiatrist to see how the campers were coping, and give us pointers on how to deal with problems. It turned out that my psychotic camper was having so much trouble adapting to the experience that the director and his wife had to take him into their cabin. Another one of my boys snored loudly and wet his bed every night, plus he was prone to seizures, which he had after lunch for the first three days of camp. I mentioned the seizure situation to the psychiatrist one night, and I told about his grand mal episodes, it turned out the kid didn't have grand mal seizures at all, and I'd been hoodwinked. I was told to call the kid's bluff the next time. Seizure boy went into his routine, and when he quit jerking around, I told my other campers that the kid was faking. When I said this, the faker opened his eyes, sat up and proudly announced that he had fooled us all. I took the gender identification boy out in a rowboat and showed him how to bait a hook, catch a fish, take the hook out of the fish's mouth and not act like a girl. This boy's parents told the camp director that the camping experiences completely turned him around and the boy said it was the neatest thing he had ever done.

For me, I was so exhausted from the experience, mainly from sleep deprivation, that when I returned home I slept nearly 24 hours straight.

The exposure to kids with special needs made me have the highest respect for teachers who chose Special Education as a teaching career. When I returned to school after my experience I interacted with the special kids in my school building to encourage them and their teachers.

I increased my salary just under $200 dollars a year, and if I didn't take another course for the next 10 years, I could advance to $8508.50 per year. That's assuming the pay schedule didn't change over that period of time – which wasn't very likely.

~11~

Subjects Taught

I assume that as a beginning teacher many schools made an effort to get the most work as they can out of their new hires – like squeezing blood from a turnip. Looking back, I'm flabbergasted by the demands of my daily schedule and wonder how I lasted one week, let alone thirty years. But adapting to a frenetic schedule under challenging circumstances was almost like competing in a mental cross-country marathon.

Some teachers specialize in one subject and may have different levels within that subject; like mathematics – algebra, geometry, trigonometry; English – grades 9-12, literature, composition, etc. I started teaching drama, speech and English 10. By the end of the year, debate was added. As the years went by, I added English 11, remedial English 10, forensics, film study, film making, media now, photography, communications, TV, success, reading, year book and video year book (17 subjects). In other words, I was a utility teacher. Other than English, every other class was an elective, which allowed me to use my creativity and enjoy my career choice.

Classes I Taught

DRAMA

[Taught for six years]

In costume as a drama teacher

The truth be told, I'm not enamored with the dramatic arts. My father played a part in the movie actor, Spencer Tracy, getting into drama in college.[3] Tracy told my father, that after getting into movies, his life was controlled by the movie industry and he was not able to live a "normal" life. He was unable to, as Shakespeare put it, "To thine own self be true." His joie de vivre was gone.

---

[3] Spencer and my dad were high school and college roommates, performing in college productions at Ripon College in 1921-22.

I took several courses in drama in college, including "Shakespeare" where I studied and viewed many of his plays. I admired the playwright's writing skills, but the idea of devoting my life to memorizing words written by a 16th century playwright just didn't "click." I came across many devotees to drama and, in particular, to Shakespeare, who seemed to lose contact with the "real world" in their devotion. I recall a skit on *Saturday Night Live* where William Shatner speaks at a Star Trek convention and says, "Get a life! For cryin' out loud, it's just a TV show!"

My involvement in the dramatic arts began in 1965 when I attended the University of Puget Sound. I was awarded a partial scholarship at the college through the Department of Speech and Drama. I was expected to build sets and props, act in small roles, be a stage hand and eventually be a stage manager. I was grateful for reduced tuition, but I'll have to admit a lack of true enthusiasm to thespian activities. Sooo much time is involved for so little production.

Musical productions grabbed me more than speaking-only plays. I enjoyed *Westside Story* more than any of the several productions I saw of *Romeo & Juliet* – *Kiss Me Kate* more than *Taming of the Shrew*. The best production I ever saw and was involved in was *The Fantasticks*. The acting and singing was superb, as were the musicians.

I found many thespian-types to be temperamental and egocentric. The unspoken words in my mind were, "it's only a play!" There were even prima donnas at the high school level who tried to sway me to choose them for roles based on unseen past performances.

My attitude about performers who thought they were better than others, developed in 1958 when I was a singer/performer with a popular college quartet. After a performance in a large Seattle theater, hundreds of girls screamed during our performance, and asked for autographs afterwards. I thought the entire scene was phony and thought, "If you knew that I am just a normal guy who knows a few chords on the banjo and can sing in key, would you treat me this way?"

Both of my drama classes were populated with many nonacademic-types, as well as some serious students. I was expected to direct the school plays and assist with a musical in the spring, so I had to keep my eyes open for actors for my first production within the next two months.

The first activity I had my classes do was a group pantomime. One group of rowdy boys did an old-time cowboy barroom brawl. In their mix was a "slow-but-good-natured" boy who agreed to get "knocked out" for the skit. Well, one of the larger boys actually knocked him out! All eyes were on me to see how I'd handle the situation. I didn't get excited, checked to see if the victim was still able to breathe (bringing to mind the mantra 'the show must go on'), and managed to keep on track with the remaining pantomimes.

The drama director who preceded me managed to write and produce plays in the spring. Evidently, because he was dramatically gifted, I was assumed to have the same abilities. I felt like *the sword of Damocles* was hanging over my head. Meanwhile, I had three different subjects to teach to five different overflowing classes, a play to direct in the fall, and my wife would be delivering a baby sometime in November. Maybe the Rapture or World War III would occur and I wouldn't have to worry about my situation. The first play I directed went off smoothly, I became a father of a daughter and I survived the large class load.

The high school's music director chose to produce the play *Mame* for the spring musical. Because of my college experience with musicals, I felt confident this production would probably come off pretty well, especially because of the high school's talented and experienced music director.

The lighting and scenery was a different story. The lights were on switches, not dimmers, and there were no professional stage lights, just 150W bulbs with two one-gallon tin cans taped together to act as unmovable spotlights. John, the music director, aka Rube Goldberg, jury-rigged a dimmer with wires running from the electrical box to a coil of wire on a broomstick which would be plunged into a 30-gallon plastic garbage can full of salt water when we wanted the stage lights to dim. Miraculously nobody was electrocuted and the setup worked! The stage presented another problem for scenery changes. Flats couldn't dropped from the flies (overhead) because large heating ducts occupied most of the space, so we had to build rolling scenery that came onto the stage from each side. The actors did a bang-up job and the music was excellent. I'm sure the audience was amazed that such a complicated production could be performed on the little stage at one end of the lunchroom. I know I was.

DEBATE & FORENSICS

[Taught for three years]

With spring coming up, I was contracted to not only to produce another play, but also coach a debate team. College prepared me to do these jobs, but I would be working with rank-amateur high school students. Just as athletic directors have to set up a schedule for sporting activities; as debate coach I had to work out a schedule with other schools in our area, plus host a couple of the competitions at our school and supply judges. About ten or twelve student signed up (five or six teams), and spent many hours preparing to debate for or against the nationwide debate topic picked by the National Forensics League. The topic was **Resolved: That Congress should establish uniform regulations to control criminal investigation procedures.**

When we traveled to another school, and didn't qualify for a school bus, because of the low body count, the school district only provided a well-traveled station wagon which I had to drive, and since there wasn't enough room for all the students and I couldn't get another driver for another vehicle, I had to have one of my students drive my wife's 1951 Chevrolet. Obviously, I didn't worry about liability or the stupidity of the situation. On a trip to a high school where I'd never visited before, I ended up driving down a steep hill which ended up on the waterfront of Port Orchard. As I descended in the station wagon, the boy driving my car, passed me. The brakes had failed! He used his head, and pulled the emergency brake, slowing just enough to avoid going into the bay. The debate didn't go very well either. Besides debate there were other speech competitions called forensics or individual speaking events. The classifications were: *impromptu* (speaking four to six minutes on a topic, single word or phrase, picked for a speaker with no preparation); *oratory* (an eight to ten minute memorized speech of the speaker's choice with the purpose to inspire or convince); *oral interpretation* (an eight minute memorized speech of non-original material); *extemporaneous speaking* (a four to seven minute speech from one of three topics – 30 minutes preparation – no notes allowed)

I'll admit that I developed a close family-like relationship with a core group of actors and debate/forensic students because so much time was spent together. Nearly 50 years later I have contact with several of these students.

The only subject I taught for 30 years

SPEECH ~ PUBLIC SPEAKING

Supposedly, the greatest fear most people have is speaking in public. I'll confess to being in that category in my grade school days. The senior pastor of a church I attend, who has been preaching for 50 years, told me that every Sunday he preaches, stage fright kicks in as soon as he faces the congregation. If he wasn't a preacher I'd accuse him of lying.

I had my first experience of speaking in public in junior high school as a campaign manager for a classmate who was running for student body president. My father gave speeches at conventions for dentists, as well as other venues, so I enlisted his help. He told me to be organized and prepare what I wanted to say beforehand, and if I practiced my delivery, I would be able to speak during my period of nervousness and eventually be able to calm down and show confidence. This advice worked and my candidate won, and compared to the other candidates' campaign speeches, mine sounded good.

When I took a speech class in high school, my teacher gave us a variety of purposes and types of speeches to perform, helping me to develop a speaking style. As in any skill, speaking to an audience became easier and easier and I discovered I was better than average. Epiphany! Finally, I was good at something besides singing, eating, sleeping, climbing trees and rowing!

Sales pitches I employed when I was a salesman came in very handy in teaching various subjects in order to "sell" the subjects I taught to my audience (students). I also used pitches to sell nontraditional subjects to the school's administrators over the years.

Like everything else, some people are naturally gifted with the ability to speak. For the majority of others, speaking in front of people is paramount to standing naked in front of a congregation of critical and clothed people. But I believed I had a method of teaching this subject that would benefit almost everyone:

Students were told to take notes on:

Purposes for speeches – Convince, Stimulate, Inform, and Entertain (definitions)

Preparation – Impromptu, Memorization and Extemporaneous (definitions)

Parts of Speech – Content (what is said) and Delivery (how it is said) [examples]

Each graded *speech was rated* on a subjective 10 Point Scale for *Content* and 10 Point Scale for *Delivery*: 10=Perfect, 9=Excellent, 8=Very Good, 7=Good, 6=Average, 5=Fair, 4=Not So Hot, 3=Needs Work, 2=Lame, 1=DOA. A speech with a score of 8/7 translates to Very Good Content/ Good Delivery. The 10 Point Rating Scale remained on one side of my chalkboard throughout the school year, and when the faculty had meetings in my room some teachers referred to it as the "Edgerian Performance Scoreboard." I can't claim credit for inventing this number grading system. It was used in the speech classes I took at the University of Puget Sound. The word description was my creation.

Divisions (Organization) of Speech - Introduction, Body and Conclusion (examples).

A quiz was then given on the information (students could use notes). The caveat was given that the same quiz would be given the next day without using notes and would be graded.

After explaining the why of stage fright (adrenalin), I told the students they would *not* be graded on the **first** two **speeches**. Most of them would be nervous, so just the experience of facing an audience they would give:

1. an *Introductory speech* of who they were, where they lived, names and ages of brothers/sisters, if they had any pets, and finally, why they were taking Speech. After each speaker was through, I kept them on their feet by asking questions about something they said, and complimented them on something in their presentation and, if necessary, I made suggestions to help in a weak area (usually volume or eye contact).

2. *Past-Present-Future*: Something interesting or entertaining from their past. What their present interests or activities involved. What they had in mind for the future and how they were preparing for it.

The following speeches required an outline (except for *Impromptu)* [typed to qualify for a 10]: A speech to *Inform,* using a *2-D* visual aid; An *Interesting Person* speech; a *3-D* visual aid (show & tell) speech; a speech to *Entertain*; a speech to *Convince* us of something; *Impromptu* (a grab bag of objects) and a *Panel Discussion*. In later years I did an *Interview* in front of the class, using their typed résumés.

MEMORABLE SPEECHES

After hearing hundreds – perhaps thousands – of speeches over the years, some still remain in my memory. The most moving speech was given by an unmarried mother who used her baby as a visual aid for a speech to convince us of why *sex avoidance* as a teenager was necessary. Another unmarried mother gave a show & tell using her baby, but it was not well thought out or delivered. The fact that the infant survived being passed around the class like a puppy made the speech memorable.

My classes and I tended to enjoy speeches involving food. A student who fished commercially brought in a large salmon which he barbequed outside; a girl whose father owned a bakery brought in a cake which she decorated and we ate; a girl whose father owned a deli made us a six-foot hoagie. Of course, there were many other food type speeches and one time a student got her finger stuck in a mixer.

An inventive boy designed an electrical worm shocker/hotdog cooker by using two separated 16-penny nails on a board which were attached to an electrical wire with a plug. The inventor said when the nails were put into the ground and plugged in, worms would come to the surface. As a hotdog cooker, the same setup was used with the nails penetrating the dog. It did quickly electrocute hotdogs, but nobody would eat one.

There was a radio commentator, Paul Harvey, who broadcast a program *News and Comments* as well as *The Rest of the Story* for the better part of 50 years. It was very popular because of a variety of offbeat stories. One story he broadcast concerned one of my speech students who had withdrawn thousands of dollars from several bank ATMs. He only had about $30.00 in his account and wanted to withdraw $20.00. When he received the cash and receipt, nothing showed on the receipt. He went on to see if he could get more money out, which he did to the point of cleaning out the machine. He went to another branch, and did the same thing. After emptying other ATMs he went home, scattered the money on the floor and rolled in it – giving meaning to the expression "rolling in dough." When he realized he had inadvertently committed bank robbery, his conscience kicked in. How would he avoid being charged with a major crime if somehow the missing money was traced to him? He gathered his monetary windfall into a garbage bag and took it to the local police and fessed-up to the inadvertent crime. The money was returned to the banks, he was not charged with a crime, and he was able to keep the original $20.00 he intended to withdraw and was also issued a new bank card.

Once, a boy told us about his misadventure with a bicycle that led to one of his toes being cut off. When he showed us the result of it being reattached, a girl in the class turned absolutely green. The sight of the toe did-her-in to the point she had to remain in the classroom 15 minutes into the next class period for fear that if she moved, she'd throw up or pass out.

Another boy told us that he was never allowed to go outside for the first four years of his life. We learned how he thought and wondered why he could see other kids playing outdoors, yet he couldn't join them. His parents told him he was different from them. He was rescued by the Child Protective Services and then was adopted by a family in our community.

One boy gave a clever speech which involved several layers of shirts with logos, that when peeled off one-at-a-time aided in the telling of an entertaining story.

Many foreign exchange student at our school took speech. A girl from Greece who had very long hair, would inevitable precede each speech by bending forward in order to have all of her hair touching the floor, then dramatically throw her head up and back so no hair was in front of her. The class and I always enjoyed the show.

I think my favorite foreign student, because of his speaking ability (thought, preparation and presentation), was a boy from New Zealand who had his sights set on becoming a lawyer. His speeches were always near perfect, and we became much more informed about his country.

Without exception, the students from Norway and Sweden spoke excellent English, and always gave good presentations.

The most interesting foreign students were two girls from Micronesia, and one from China, who came to the U.S. via a South Vietnamese Refugee Camp. It was fascinating to hear how they reacted and adapted to a life so different from theirs.

An unspoken but strictly adhered-to rule adopted by my speech classes was, "If you don't want this information to leave this classroom, say, *'This is off the record!'" (Mum's the word)*. As far as I know this caveat was adhered to, and many were the times I had to bite my tongue when the information was concerning teachers or students. It was as if I was their conscience, and sometimes I had to inject my thoughts or feelings. Also, I was able to keep current with what was important in their lives. In a way, I became one of them.

As a speech teacher I was asked to perform Master of Ceremonies duties for various occasions such as assemblies, banquets, presentations, etc. When the valedictorian or other students gave a speech at graduation, I'd be the advisor. Once, I was picked to be the person to read the names of the graduating class, and eventually selected as the graduation speaker - which I started doing in 1974, then in the 80s and 90s – six times.

FILM STUDY/FILMMAKING

[Taught for 25 years]

In 1969 there was no such thing as video. In order to watch action, it was necessary to watch 8mm (home movies) or 16mm educational or sports films. As I recall, one-day-a-week, there was a 20-minute segment of time called Activity Period where students could engage in some activity for a club, society, etc. A colleague who was a math and history teacher came up with an activity to make an 8mm movie. Although many students showed interest, nothing much came of it. I thought there was potential in offering a class called Film Study. I had taken many films of my travels in the Far East and had learned how to edit and splice film and use expensive and complex movie cameras when I was in the service, and our local public library had a large collection of 8mm films that were available to be viewed at home. When our principal sought out subject areas we might offer for future classes, I pointed out the interest in the filmmaking activity. I laid out a plan for such a class; it was approved and I was off and running with a class that attracted the attention of many students. Since our class would be making silent films, there were many older silent films that were used as examples of filmmaking techniques. Most students became familiar with the names of silent screen film stars such as Douglas Fairbanks, Bronco Billy, Pearl White, Tom Mix, Mary Pickford, Buster Keaton, Charlie Chaplin et al., so the films we watched were also a look into the history of filmmaking. Movie terminology and techniques were emphasized in order to prepare the students to make their own movies. From the start, the film study class proved to be popular, and only seniors could take the class. A fee was charged to cover the cost of film, equipment and processing. The class (often over 40 – in one case 52) was split into groups, given an 8mm camera and a 50-foot (3 ½ min.) roll of film, and an assignment sheet of what to film. The final edited film was shown to all my classes. In one instance a School Board member came to my class to find out what was required of the students, then came back to see the finished product.

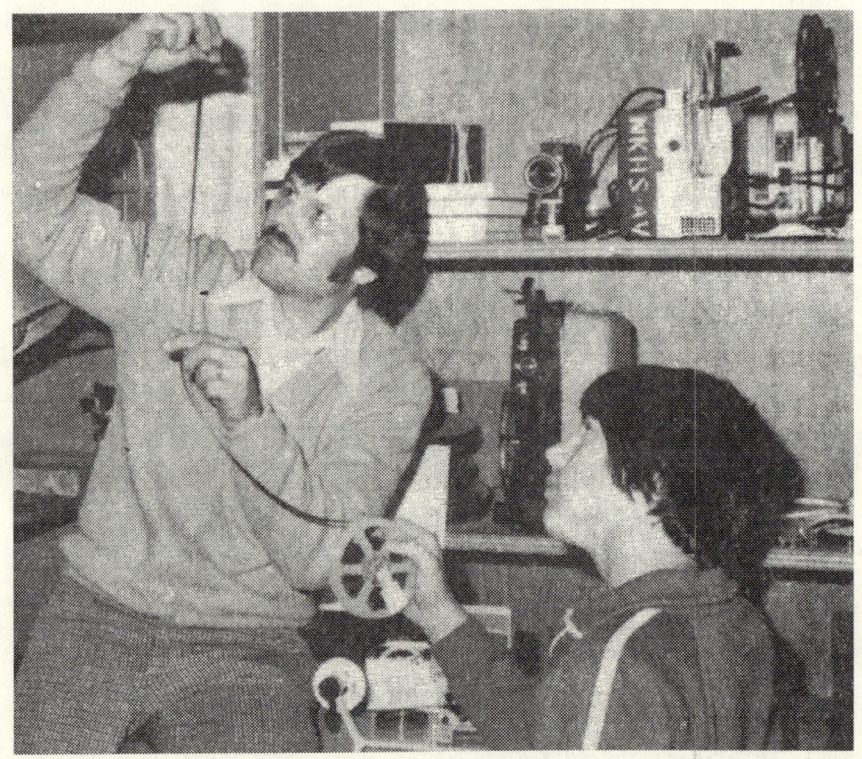

Working with a film student

Eventually, the class evolved into a class that filmed, processed and used
some complicated movie equipment. Once students had mastered basic
techniques, they were required to make an independently scripted and
produced film. Some of these films were shown during lunchtime for
a fee. During these movie-making years, a few students earned honors
in state student filmmaking contests, and some went into film and TV
careers. One student, John Goheen, won the National Press Photographer
Association's Television News Photographer of the Year, three-years-in-
a-row, claiming to have gotten interested in his craft in the film study/
filmmaking class in the 1970s. Another student submitted an animated
8mm film to the Walt Disney Animation School and was accepted on the
basis of that film. The class also was a stress-relieving activity that was
interesting, informative and enjoyable.

A boy (Dave A.) in an early film study class, made a successful film
with a title taken from a compilation movie called *The Saga of William*

S. Hart (a western star in silent films), calling his film *The Saga of Paul P.* The movie proved to be very popular, so Dave suggested that we have movie awards for best student films, called the *Edgar* (loosely based on my last name). The award presented was a garage sale-acquired trophy for a dog show (Best Tri-color) with a statue of a dog on top. When word got out to the community, I received donations of trophies of every sport or activity that ever presented a trophy, from people who had old trophies in their attic, garage or closet. For the remaining 20 years of teaching I had so many trophies that I gave them for performances in any class I taught. I would have students vote for whom they thought deserved them.

Dave also suggested making a 16mm sound movie with him as the camera man and an actor based on the subject of hitchhiking. He hitchhiked to college and back home, about 30-miles, every day. We wrote a script on a paper napkin, cast two faculty members and him as the characters. My car and a borrowed 16mm camera were used and we spent about two months putting it all together. Actually, the 10-minute color/BW film, *The Perfect Hitchhiker*, turned out pretty good, and we both learned a great deal about making a sound movie. We made this movie while I was pursuing a Master's Degree, and I had to select a topic for my thesis. My high school film classes were making animated films using drawings, clay, cutouts and 3-D objects, but I was unable to find any film to show a variety of animation techniques. I submitted my proposal to make an instructive film dealing with various techniques that could be done by amateurs with home movie equipment. The finished 17-minute, Color/B&W, sound film was titled *An Animation Sampler*. The film was well received, and was made into a VHS video tape which was available for use in all schools from our Kitsap County Media Resource Center and also available to four other counties. I used the film at a Statewide Conference, in various schools, and in one case I showed the film at an assembly. A little interest and knowledge went a long way.

SUCCESS

[Taught for my last six years]

I had two-hours-a-day while driving to and from work when I could listen to news, books on tape, and other subjects on tape. I checked out some tapes by a man named Earl Nightingale (Nightingale-Conant Corporation) who put out a monthly publication called *Insight* (booklet and audio cassette), aimed at motivation which presented ideas and stories to inspire or motivate listeners. I went on to request a catalogue from the company, and found many other motivational-type speakers on a variety of topics. As I listened to these tapes I discovered many ideas that I could incorporate in many of my classes, and I eventually discovered many other audio, video and written sources that might be used in a class to help motivate students to do better in school as well as in life in general. Once again I pitched my class idea to the principal and curriculum committee as an offering to students for an elective subject. I received an okay, and the new course was off and running. The course proved to be quite successful, and was offered as a subject for the last five years of my teaching in public school.

I also had an opportunity to take a weeklong class and workshop called Keys to Motivation® which I was required to teach (as an adjunct professor) to teachers for five hours of college credit. There were many ideas on motivation I was able to use in my high school success class. I combined all my resources into a class taught in a class for teachers offered through the Heritage Institute/Antioch University, called Keys to Success.

MEDIA NOW

[Taught for 15 years]

This media literacy class was offered to teacher through our Educational Service District which offered five hours of college credit for a 50-hour (weeklong) workshop. Those teachers who were accepted as students would be instructed in how to teach this nationwide curriculum. When we finished the course training, we had to submit a proposal to our school district for grant funding (several thousand dollars) for equipment, supplies and workbooks needed to launch the program. Fortunately, the school district superintendent and I got along well, and he understood the value of such a course, so I received funds and offered the class as an elective subject.

The students were provided with workbooks, media kits, and had access to a variety of equipment needed for class and individual activities involving media. I had to explain and demonstrate how each activity was accomplished. For example for photography, I had to explain the camera's features, how to load the film in the camera, how to compose and light the subject (portrait), place the exposed film in a developing tank, use chemicals for developing film. Next, the film was placed in an enlarger and exposed to photographic paper and finally printed.

After teaching the course, teachers who taught Media Now were asked how we would change or improve the activities in the workbooks. I found that I would change or tweak just about every activity. When the Media Now program support was ended, teachers were told that if they wanted to continue teaching the course, they could purchase whatever workbooks were left in stock for $10. This expense would have to come from charging my students for taking the class. Most students abided and the class continued up to the time the workbook provider ran out of stock. I had all the supplies and equipment for the class, but if I wanted to continue with the course, I'd have to design my own version of the workbook. So, I spent most of one summer laying out my tweaked version of the workbooks. I had all the pages printed out and laid out for each student to put together as their own workbook. This reminded me of my 5th grade teacher's project of putting together a class book.

~12~

Bumps and Adjustments

During the years I taught in the high school, there were several changes in the structure of the classroom day. We had semesters, quarters and trimesters (12 weeks). Most of those years there was a six-period day, but in my last two years, the high school went to a four-period-day, called the Block System. My classroom subjects were pared down to Speech, Film Study/Media Now and Success.

Because of Maintenance and Operation Levy failures, funds were cut and (especially in Debate) the program which was built upon a group of students who were building on experience and practice would suddenly not have the activity available to them. After three levy failures, I threw in the towel and let somebody else in the community or school district pick up this activities when funds became available. Eventually, (after 13 years) English disappeared from my teaching schedule because my class load increased in other classes I taught. Some of the classes I instructed, like photography, were taught by the Vocational Education Department when classroom buildings and facilities were built.

In 1989-90 the State changed the requirements for college course credits earned before receiving a B.A. counting for credit on the Statewide Salary Schedule. I had five years to go before retirement, which meant, in my case, 45 hours of credits would have to be made up. After I took a one-credit (10 hours of class time) class, I wrote the following letter:

December 3, 1990

To Whom It May Concern:

I just spent 10 hours in a class (my 102nd college course) that took me an hour and a half to drive to, and requires me to write a paper in order to get one hour of credit at a cost of $54. The required book for the class costs $12.50 and takes five or six hours to read. Next weekend I get to spend 20 hours in a class that will take me about four hours to drive to, plus I'll have to spend two nights in a motel. All this will get me two hours of credit. The weekend after that I've got another 20 hours in classes, and I have to drive to Olympia one day and Seattle the next – and so it goes until I recoup the 45+ 'soft credits' of pre B.A. credits that were snatched away from me as though they were a figment of my imagination.

I have already spent thousands of hours and thousands of dollars taking over 100 college classes at first-rate universities. But **now** that's not good enough to qualify for credit on the (*New*) Statewide Salary Schedule. These **hard-earned** credits I've taken at the University of Washington, University of Puget Sound, Seattle Pacific University, Eastern Washington State University, University of Maryland Overseas and other universities and colleges before I graduated and became a teacher are classified as 'soft credits' along with such fluff as taking district first aid classes, being on the District Reading Committee, and probably reviewing movies on trench foot, etc. Why in the world are these latter named 'softies' classified the same as college classes like Educational Statistics, Accounting, Economics or Pacific Northwest History? **THIS IS COMPARING APPLES TO BELLY BUTTON LINT!**

Needless to say, I ABSOLUTELY DO NOT SEE, NOR WILL I EVER UNDERSTAND THE EQUATING OF DISTRICT CREDITS OR CLASSES WITH COLLEGE CLASSES!

I'm registered to take a course this month on Kenya, which no doubt will be educational and interesting, that simply satisfies the requirement of a post B.A. credit. I took a class through the University of Washington on learning how to set up and teach classes in Media, which I've been teaching two times a day for the past 10 years – BUT – I didn't take the class for credit because I didn't need the credit! Now, the rules are changed and I don't need credit for something I've done. I've even published a workbook for this class for which I don't get credit. Another irony in this soft and hard credit and the rule change is that I'll get credit for something I'll never teach or use (Kenya), but not get credit for something I've taken and teach twice a day.

The way the requirements are written, I can take the exact same classes I took prior to receiving my B.A. *now* and get credit for it, but because I took the class before these new regulations were written they don't count! **WAIT A MINUTE!** This is **UNFAIR, TOTALLY ASININE, ILLOGICAL, etc. adinfinitum!** What difference does it make when I took a class? Does it change the fact that I took it? That's like telling me that the first time I took it was just for practice, but now it counts.

Don Edgers

M. Ed. +90, Step 15

Of course I got little satisfaction from writing this letter other than I was able to let off a little steam. I spent 450 hours taking mostly useless courses in order to maintain my status on the salary schedule.

Unfortunately, some teachers with only a year left until retirement didn't have time to recover lost credit. Then there were others who just didn't have the time or money to enable them to makeup the lost credit.

The purpose of this regulation by the State was no doubt a ploy to reduce the costs of the education budget.

FACILITIES

At first glance, in 1967, the 10-year-old brick building where I would spend the next 28 years, appeared well kept. There were also smaller brick buildings which housed industrial arts classes, a gymnasium and a music building. The only eyesore was the student dirt parking lot, which appeared to be remnants of a WWI battlefield.

Overcrowded classrooms were the norm in most of the schools I attended, even in college. However, the worst case was in the first years at the high school where I taught. I felt like an indoor-peripatetic, like Aristotle, who taught philosophy while walking in the Lyceum of ancient Athens. The only time I taught in one room or place more than one time a day was in 1969. Shortly before school started I had broken one foot and the cast was set at an angle that wouldn't allow me to walk with a walking cast. Tethered to crutches made it virtually impossible to carry books and papers to various far-flung rooms. My disability meant that I was able to command one room all day – that is, until I didn't have to use crutches anymore. I longed for the day when I didn't have to wander the hallways in search of a room. The next year a building with 14 additional classrooms was built and my wandering came to an end. The room I had was next to the stage, which I had to use for classes with more than 30 students or when I wanted to show films. The classroom had two walls of windows plus a skylight. I didn't dare complain because at least I had a room I could call home.

A few years later a new facility for Music, Drama, a swimming pool and a restaurant was built across the road from the high school, along with a new junior high school. The Music Building was vacated, and I put in a request to move in. It was perfect for the classes I taught. One problem was the lack of desks or chairs, a problem that was solved by the junior high principal who gave me a key to the vacated old junior high school, with permission to collect anything I needed from the classrooms. The new junior high school was furnished with all new furnishings, so the old-but-useable furniture was available to me for the taking. I made several trips in my pickup truck until I refurnished *my* new facility.

Some problems occurred during my tenure in the building for more than 20 years, like a very leaky roof, electrical lighting failure (not good in a building with no windows) and a burst pipe due to freezing and thawing during a Christmas break. The roof and lighting problems were due to the lack of maintenance staffing because of repeated Maintenance & Operations levy failures. The only reasons these problems were addressed were because a student slipped on a wet floor, jamming a pencil into his hand, and when faculty meetings were held in my room the principal complained that only half of the lights were operational. The students in my classes referred to one side of the room where most of the lights didn't work as 'the dark side.'

One of my students was a projectionist at a local drive-in and downtown movie theater, and asked me if I wanted movie posters that were piling up in the projection rooms, with which to decorate the new classroom. Posters filled up nearly every wall (there were no windows) in the building and created a Disneyland-like spectacle to anyone entering the room. When new posters came in, I covered the old ones. Sometimes students who heard about the posters, but weren't in my classes would come into the room to examine them like spectators at an art gallery.

Before I had the old music building for my classes, I was on the lookout for teaching positions closer to my home, but afterwards, I put that thought out of my mind. I honestly looked forward to teaching in my spacious and multifunctional facility – leaky roof and all.

~13~

Graduate School

[1973-1975]

After teaching for six years, I returned to the University of Washington during summer quarter in order to take courses in order to advance on the pay scale in my school district. Some classes I took were in the area of film study (history, genres, directors, actors, etc.) and film making.

I had pioneered film study/filmmaking classes using 8mm film three years after beginning my teaching career, and the classes proved to be very popular. It's necessary to remember that in the 1960s and 1970s video was not available, so home movies were the primary way to preserve moving memories.

The courses I took turned out to be interesting and useful, plus they were listed as subjects qualifying in a Master of Education program titled Learning Resources. I qualified for Veteran's Administration tuition assistance until 1975 if I was accepted into a graduate program and took the required coursework. The writing was on the wall, so to speak, and if I wanted to get a Master's Degree, dilly-dallying wasn't an option.

In January of 1973 the following response to my request to be admitted to graduate school was received from The Graduate School, Office of the Dean:

Dear Mr. Edgers:

Your application for admission to the Graduate School of the University of Washington has been given special consideration, and *I am sorry to have to inform you* (italics mine) that it will not be possible to admit you at this time.

The primary criterion for admission is the apparent ability of the applicant, as decided by the University to proceed with his proposed program. Evidence of the applicant's ability is obtained from a review of the prior academic records of his undergraduate preparation in the field of his interest, and from other pertinent sources.

We regret that in some fields the University is unable to accept all qualified applicants because more apply than can be properly accommodated and so availability of sufficient faculty and facilities become additional consideration.

I hope you will be able to develop alternate plans to achieve the objectives you desire.

Yours very sincerely,
J.L.M
Dean

After pondering this punch-in-the-gut letter, I used my experience as a debate coach to counter every reason (times 10) given for being rejected in a two-page letter. A short time later I received a letter saying, "Dear Mr. Edgers: Your application for the degree of Master of Education has been approved by the Dean of the Graduate School --------------------- Yours very sincerely, J.L.M., Dean of the Graduate School."

A list of required and elective classes along with the required number of hours needed to complete the degree requirements became my guide for the next two years. Classwork was needed every single quarter, including summers, in order to receive financial aid from the Veteran's Administration.

Fortunately, some classes I had taken in the film related subjects counted towards the hours required in graduate school even though I took them before being accepted. When I was in the Army I took a course in Educational Statistics in anticipation of returning to college to get a teaching degree. The same course, using the same book was a graduate school requirement, so I took it over and, wouldn't you know it, educational statistics information hadn't changed! I discovered from fellow grad students this was a dreaded course requirement, especially for the mathematically challenged.

One 500-level class required by all students was taught by a professor who might as well have been lecturing in Sanskrit, based on his vocabulary. This professor, a doctor, lectured for an hour and a half before taking a break. His abnormally superior vocabulary was so mind boggling I had no idea what he was talking about. I felt so confused that I seriously thought about bagging graduate school. Fortunately, as I was walking out of the classroom I overheard two students who said, "Do you have any idea what he (the prof.) was talking about?"

"I don't have a clue."

With this little exchange, I decided to tough it out. It turned out that each class member would pick from a list of subject and a date to lecture to us. I seem to recall there were four lectures per class session. The prof. did give us a take-home midterm, and it was necessary to use a dictionary to translate his terminology into understandable English.

My thesis actually was a 20-minute, 16mm film titled *An Animation Film Sampler* and showed all available types of animated films and how to make them. The script and storyboard were placed in the University's library, and the film was copied onto videotape and made available to five different county school districts. I used the film to show at assemblies and workshops, and got schools who might be interested in this sort of thing to actually use the information.

One of my students won first place in a Washington State Student Film Competition with an animated apple (pixilated) film called *Hard Core*. It didn't hurt that his dad was the president of the school board.

Another student was accepted by the Walt Disney School because of a cel animated film he submitted. He actually went to the school, but decided on a career as a fine artist instead.

I received my Master of Education degree on June 14, 1975, signed by the President of the University, President of the Board of Regents and the Dean who'd rejected my application to Graduate School two years before.

~14~

Master Commuter

Over my 28 years of commuting, I spent over 8,000 hours in 19 different vehicles. I came across many interesting people in the form of passengers, drivers and hitchhikers and experienced many traveling situations while in a car or on a bus.

I saw bad accidents, was in minor ones, had heart-stopping close calls, watched bizarre drivers in action, yet lived to tell the tale.

Not only did the traffic increased significantly over the years, the roads and highways improved. When I first began my daily trek on a two-lane highway with no stoplights or stop signs and a 55 mile-per-hour speed limit for about half of that distance, the commute took me one hour. Eventually there was a four-lane freeway 85% of the way, but four stoplights, and it still took me an hour. So, with all the road improvements over the years, I drove all those miles at 45-miles per hour, except in snowy weather.

Somewhere I read that if you do something for an hour a day you can become an expert in that area in five years. My apprenticeship as a commuter began in September of 1967 when I started commuting two hours-a-day, or 90 miles, for 28 years. After that I drove about 1½ hours, or 35-miles-a-day for two years. This not only qualified me as an expert, but also a nonpaid professional.

Obviously, the expenses required with so much traveling required me to learn how to maintain my vehicles which included: a 1951 Chevrolet, '55 Chevrolet, '61 Ford, '61 Volkswagen, two different '65 Fords, '65 Dodge, '66 Opel, '67 Plymouth, '68 Cadillac, '69 Plymouth, '69 Opel, '69 Ford pickup, '72 Plymouth, '72 Volkswagen, '77 Opel, '79 Honda, '79 Datsun pickup, and a 1987 Toyota pickup. The ones I drove the most were the '61 Ford, '61 Volkswagen, two different '65 Fords, '66 Opel, '79 Honda, '79 Datsun, and until 1997 the 1987 Toyota pickup.

BEST VALUES

One of the best deals was a 1961 Ford, Galaxy 500 convertible with under 70,000 miles, with leather upholstery that I bought from a colleague who was its original owner for $150. I sold it three years later to another colleague for $125, and all I had to replace was a water pump and a muffler. The best deal was a 1968 Cadillac that I got in 1982 for free from my mom when she was 82. Admittedly, this fine vehicle wasn't used very often for commuting unless the roads were really bad and I needed the studded snow tires and extra weight. This car made me sort of nervous because it was so luxurious. Since my personality doesn't let me show off without feelings embarrassed, I sold this vehicle three years later to a neighbor.

WORST VALUES

I came to regard a new car as absolutely the worst investment for commuting. I've bought three new cars: The first was a 1967 Plymouth Fury III, two-door sedan with an eight-cylinder 318 cubic-inch engine with an automatic transmission. It cost me slightly under $3000, with the exception of having to replace the rear axle because of a growl that developed in the first couple of years. When I went to sell that car, with it still new looking and running great, it had close to 100,000 miles on it, after three years, I was lucky to get $600!

The second new vehicle I got for about $4000 was a 1977 Opel Kadett with air-conditioning. It was a four-door with a four-speed stick shift and a pretty decent car, but had horrendously squeaky brakes, and since I got stung on the 1967 Plymouth I decided to sell it before it got too much mileage. The people who ended up buying it came over to look at it one night. I backed it out of the garage so they could see it better, and then drove it back into the garage, leaving the keys in the ignition. I parked my 1966 Opel behind it with the keys in it, also. I didn't think anything about leaving the keys in the cars as we lived on a private road and had never heard of any car being stolen from Fox Island.

TWO CARS STOLEN ONE NIGHT

About 2:00 AM, our phone rang and a sheriff asked me if I'd given permission to a neighbor boy to drive our 1977 Opel, because if I hadn't, I'd better come and get it on a road under the Tacoma Narrows Bridge. I woke up my wife and daughter so we could go pick up the car. The 1966 Opel also was missing. Fortunately, I also had a '69 Ford pickup truck which we drove to get the car, knowing that nobody but a fool would steal the older Opel. When we got to the place where the car was located, there was the other car. Apparently, the neighbor boy brought a friend with him and they were going to drive them to death on the power line road, but before they reached their destination they drove the '66 Opel through a large puddle and drowned it. Both car thieves were trying to get it restarted when two sheriffs came upon them and checked out the registration and gave me the 2:00 AM call. One of the sheriffs told me I probably wouldn't be able to get the drowned Opel started since the boys were having so much trouble, but it roared to life and I commuted to school the next morning and several hundred more times after that. I ended up selling the newer Opel about a week later to the people who looked at it the night it was stolen. I don't think they ever knew that someone almost got it for free.

My third new car was a 1979 Honda accord with a five speed transmission. Total cost was just under $5000 - a great little car. It was the best designed auto I've ever owned. Plus, it was comfortable and economical and it ran on leaded or unleaded gas. In snowy weather the drive felt safe because of the front-wheel-drive with studded snow tires. The car would take me anywhere without causing me to drive like a granny with tunnel vision when a snow and ice storm came.

One day as I was driving toward home, the Honda just shut down. The starter tried to engage while I was driving along and tore off a few teeth in the flywheel. A mechanic friend of mine who had a tow truck came to my rescue. I had him put in a new clutch and timing belt while it was apart. The total bill was over $500. I saw that the car had reached a point where I'd have to spend more and more money on maintenance so I decided to sell. I got a little under half of what I'd originally paid for the car after driving it six years so I didn't do too badly. Unless I somehow might come into some "big bucks", this would be our last new car.

USED CARS

Obviously a car was an important and practical part of my life but not the ruling object of my reason to exist. My main focus was engine maintenance, brakes and tires. Other than occasionally washing the vehicle and sometimes waxing, the vehicle was on its own. Whoever got a car from me got a well-maintained vehicle that had an oil and filter change religiously every 2500 miles. I had a friend in college who, in his late 20s, told me he honestly had never changed the oil in any car that he'd ever owned and probably never would have if I hadn't said something to him about it. He said he thought you were supposed to add oil when it got down.

NEW VERSUS USED CARS

I'll briefly harp on new cars and their costs before moving on. I think it was George Lucas, the director of the movie *Star Wars*, who said he thought when he bought one of the most expensive cars made he thought the vehicle would be almost repair free. He learned this wasn't true as it broke down as often as inexpensive ones. The repair bills were actually comparable to the cost of some new cars. He sold his expensive auto and bought a vehicle he could maintain.

TRAFFIC TICKETS

One might think I've gotten my share of traffic tickets over the years, but when it comes to fines for speeding, I'm a fast learner, not a fast driver. I got one a block from my school as I was driving home one night and the local police using their brand-new radar got me going 37 in a 25 MPH zone. I contributed $20 towards its purchase. When I paid my fine the fact sunk in that I had absolutely nothing to show for my money. I vowed that I'd never throw my money down a rat hole again by speeding. A fast driving colleague of mine managed to stuff that radar-speeding rat hole with many $20 bills within 30 minutes by getting two hefty speeding tickets while being clocked by an airplane both going and coming on the same highway.

I was pulled over another time and knew I wasn't speeding, so asked the patrolman, "What's up?" he came unglued. "You almost caused a major accident and you ask what's up?!" Apparently, the officer saw me pass a car going about 10 miles under the limit, but as I got abreast of the man's car, he decided to pull onto the shoulder of the road and stayed there until the patrolman came alongside him and then decided to pull onto the road again forcing the patrol car into oncoming traffic. I saw in my rearview mirror that he barely made it onto the right side of the road before having a head-on collision. The next thing I knew, I was being pulled over and made his day by asking him what was up. The trooper told me his version of what happened and I told him my version. I guess he realized his error. He shoved my driver's license back rather abruptly saying, "You just better be careful because I'll be watching for you!" Maybe that's why I drove so carefully when traveling in that segment of my commute ever after, but I don't think I saw him after that.

Other patrolmen mistakenly stopped me for driving with my parking lights; for one tail light out; twice for driving with one headlight; once for no license tab that was there; once for a loud muffler that wasn't and one time for following too closely (which I was, because a driver passed me, then slowed down because he saw a trooper's car behind him). The net result of all these times of being pulled over and maybe one or two others was that one little warning ticket was given to me for actually having a headlight out. The rest were verbal warnings or apologies.

ON TIME NO MATTER THE VEHICLE OR WEATHER

In all the years of commuting to Poulsbo, I think I was late to work two times in more than 4000 trips. Several times I made the entire trip, only to learn school had been called off (before cell phones). One windy trip, the Hood Canal Floating Bridge floated off and it took two years to rebuild it. I, like the post man with his appointed rounds to keep, got through no matter what.

Gas prices over the years (1967-1997) rose from 26.9 cents per gallon to $1.26.9 per gallon, and I went from knowing next-to-nothing about auto repair to the point of completely overhauling my 1966 Opel, and even replacing its four-speed transmission *three times*! In order to learn how to do mechanical stuff, which I really didn't like to do, my brother-in-law who lived just down the road for over 20 years, and I took an auto tune-up and repair class *three times* to make certain we didn't miss anything. Actually, we managed to keep some pretty shaky vehicles on the road over the years.

ROAD KILLS

During the springtime an unpleasant, but common, sight on the highways and roads are dead animals. The usual dogs and cats are occasionally augmented by raccoons, various rodents, lots of birds now and then, and twice I've seen cows, one being butchered. I didn't see the animals that left four-lanes of blood and gore at the half-way point of my commute, but later learned two horses escaped their confines, wandered onto the highway and met their doom when two separate 18-wheelers sent them to Kingdom Come.

Speaking of gore, I got behind a rendering truck full-to-the-brim of slaughterhouse stuff, as it was going up an incline, and because I was following too close, got blood spilled on the hood and windshield of my car.

The principal of our school parked his wife's badly damaged VW in his parking spot one day. The windshield had a hole on the passenger side with blood both inside and outside of the car. She had hit a deer and its head went through the windshield and the body went off to the side.

My vehicles have taken out several pounds of insects, a few birds, but fortunately no large animals were killed over the years. I ran over a cat but the tires missed it; a deer ran into the side of my '67 Plymouth during a snowstorm when we were moving very slowly; an Irish wolfhound ran into the side of our '72 Mercedes while it was looking in another direction - but that's it.

Probably the strangest thing I've seen dead in its tracks was a car that was upside down on the road. Since I was the first person on the scene, I stopped and asked the fellow standing next to it if I could help. He wasn't hurt, and the car didn't seem to have any dents or scratches on its sides. The whole thing looked like a set up for *Candid Camera*. I told the guy I'd give him a ride to a phone so he could call a wrecker, but Just as he was going to get into my car he said, "Just a minute!" and he crawled into an open window of the driver's side. As he backed out of the window, another car drove up. I asked the upside-down-car guy what he needed in his car and he held up his keys. He must have thought somebody might steal it while he was gone. As it turned out the upside down car's owner drove off in the other car that came along, so I never did find out how it got on its top. When I came home in the evening there was no sign that the entire incident ever happened. It was probably aliens from space, or something like that, except I think "it" was driving a Pontiac or Olds.

GAS

In the early days of my commute there wasn't much competition on gas prices. As I recall, it varied from 26.92 to 31.9 with one cent per gallon difference if you wanted regular or Ethyl®, premium, supreme, etc. Gulf Oil came up with a blend of half premium/half regular, but I guess this didn't boost their business much as they pulled out of Washington State lock, stock and oil barrel.

One time I figured how much I paid for gas per day, and it came out to a $1. 25 - $1. 50, depending on who had the cheapest gas, and I've been buying gas for the cheapest price ever since.

SERVICE STATIONS

Remember the days when gas stations were called service stations? Did I dream this, or weren't there service station attendants with uniforms that not only filled up your tank, but washed your windshield, checked your oil and air pressure in your tires? After paying six dollars for a 20 gallon tank of gas you got a four-piece setting of China (which we're still using in 2016), silverware, spices, utensils for the kitchen, or glassware, plus some S & H Green stamps! My favorite glasses (smoked ones with handles) were free with a 16 gallon fill-up from a Mobile station in Silverdale. If I made two round trips it was just right to get 17 or 18 gallons of gas and a free glass. Or you could buy the glass for $.79 with a lesser gas purchase. I managed to get 10 of them before the station was torn down. At another gas station, a Shell Service Station in Purdy, the owner apologized for just giving away Glasses. He said, "You would think they'd fill it up with peanut butter or something, wouldn't you?"

Self-service stations came about in the 1980s when I wrote, "Nowadays while I search for a squeegee in a bucket full of dirty water to clean off the windshield, the attendant glares at me and asks, 'What pump are you on, and what's your license number?' In the 1990s I was paying good money for an insulated coffee cup that had the gas company's name printed on the outside that would rub off and stick to your fingers after a week or two.

GAS SHORTAGE

During the 1973 Arab-Israeli War, Arab members of the Organization of Petroleum Exporting Countries (OPEC) imposed an oil shipment embargo against the United States to punish the U.S. decision to supply oil to the Israeli military and to gain leverage in the post-war peace negotiations. Arab OPEC members: Iraq, Iran, United Arab Emirates, Saudi Arabia and several other OPEC member countries extended the embargo to countries that supported Israel.

My commute was drastically affected because gas stations couldn't get their normal supplies of fuel. Stations had to ration the amount of gas customers could buy and limit the hours of operation, which led to long lines of cars waiting to get the fuel they needed. One station I went to, operated in the dark and conducted business by flashlight. Another station by my school opened during the time of my second period planning period, so I had to give my first period Teacher Assistant my car keys to get my car in line. I was able to run down the hill from to the station to relieve my TA, get my 10 gallons and return to school.

Gas prices continued to rise, and the hassle of gas lines were putting a dent in my patience, so I took my pickup to a farm supply store and bought their last 300 or 400 gallon storage tank, bought a hand pump with a hose and gas nozzle and set up my own gas station behind my garage. A gas truck would fill up my tank whenever it ran low.

NERVE-RACKING EXCURSIONS

Some commutes were more adventurous than others, but I had some wintertime trips when I was so nervous that my gluteus maximus or rear-end muscles were so tightened for so long that I I'd get a cramp in them. This usually happened on icy or snow-packed roads, especially as I'd go by cars off the side of the road or are sitting in the median at odd angles with their lights on. What really upset me was seeing cars pulled over and a group of people looking down a steep bank. Somehow I knew all these folks weren't looking for a Christmas tree in the same place. Fortunately, there was only one time when I got involved in an accident because of snow. I was in the '67 Plymouth and didn't have snow tires. I had to go up a slight hill of about 200 yards. I got a run at the hill and was closing in on a slow-moving bus about 100 yards in front of me. The bus had to stop for a passenger, so I slowed as much as possible without losing traction. When the bus tried to get going once again it moved forward. The only problem with this was that when the bus's tires stopped spinning, the weight of the bus bumped into me and my car managed to stop the bus, but caused me to slide backwards for another 20 feet. No major damage was done, but I had to go back all the way to the bottom of the hill and try again. This time I was successful, but the ol' buns really cramped up on me.

I usually listened to the radio for school closures early in the morning, but sometimes I didn't hear that my school was closed until I'm almost 20 miles into my commute. If I had to get on the highway and the snowplows were out, it was difficult to get turned around. This situation happened one time, and even though I had heard my school was closed, I was 10 miles into my trip, but couldn't turn back for another 20 miles. My "snow car" for this trip was a '55 Chevrolet with a stick shift, which was great in the snow. So much snow got in and under the car that only with great difficulty could I get the gear shift lever into low or reverse. Because I left the car outside upon returning home, I made the mistake of putting on the emergency brake. It froze so I couldn't drive forward until it thawed out several days later. Fortunately school had been called off during this time.

A few times I made the entire trip, only to have school closed after I've gotten there. In 1985 the snow came after school was in session. But, by the time I left at 10:30 it was impossible to get down the hill from my school to the highway. I couldn't stop without sliding onto the highway, plus several cars who tried earlier were in the ditches. The situation didn't look very encouraging as I started off in my '65 Ford with an automatic transmission and very questionable recapped, studded snow tires – their third season. I tried to work my way to the highway via 20 minutes of back roads I'd never driven. Just before reaching a small hill going to the highway there was a group of cars all stopped and looking at a vehicle in a ditch 20 feet from the highway. I decided to go for it, since it was snowing to beat the band and it would take me about an hour and a quarter on a good day from where I was to my home. As I sat there worrying whether I could make it wasn't helping my butt muscles. The old Ford made it with nary a slip, and continued for another two hours before "losing it" just a little as I was going up the hill by the Purdy's Treatment Center for Women. Just about this time on the radio I heard the announcer say, "The Tacoma Narrows Bridge is now closed!" Four miles from home I had to take three runs at a little hill before I made it to the top. The last mile to home involves getting over a hill that somebody placed a sign on that says *Fox Pass - elevation 269 feet*. Miraculously I made it over the Pass with no problem. My total time for this commute was about 2 1/2 hours.

WRECKS

- One morning as I neared the end of a two-lane 55 mph highway and slowed to 35, I came around a curve and was greeted by the sight of at least 10 road flares neatly placed on the shoulder just before a "wicked curve" and then traffic lights. As I came around the corner of the "wicked curve," There were so many fire engines, emergency aid cars and police type cars, I wasn't able to count them, and I almost didn't see the reason why they were all there. In the few seconds I could gawk and avoid a head-on collision with another gawking motorist who was been waived on by gawking sheriffs, I was able to see a totally demolished (to the point of no recognition as to the make) car, somebody in the stretcher and I think another smashed car midst what seemed like 100 flashing lights.

• I was stopped at a stoplight in Silverdale, about 15 miles from my school in Poulsbo. A Volkswagen bug was in a left turn lane next to me, when a car traveling at a speed too fast to make a right turn from a cross-road suddenly made the turn on two wheels. When the moving car's wheels were on the ground, it headed right towards us, hitting the bug head-on. The big car backed up and then sped into an embankment and got stuck in a ditch. While I ran over to the stuck car, other drivers on the scene checked out the bug's driver who was bleeding from a head wound. The driver of the accident-causing car was blasted out of his mind at about 7:00 in the morning.

• Another two-wheel, out-of-control vehicle (a ten-wheel dump truck carrying bales of scrap metal) almost rolled, while losing bales from his load, while I was stopped at a stop light at a cross road. The truck was out of control coming down a hill, honking his horn to warn any cross traffic that stopping was not an option. Normally at this time in the late afternoon there would be a fair amount of traffic, but this day there wasn't any. The truck attempted to turn the corner, and actually lifted the tires off the road on one side. This was when the metal bales scattered down the highway.

• In the late afternoon of my trip home one day as I was about 2/3 of the way home in moderate traffic, an oncoming car came sailing off the upper level of a 20 foot berm and miraculously missed the traffic on my side of the highway, then crashed into a bank on our side. The driver, who wasn't wearing a seatbelt, managed to smack his head into the car's windshield, had fallen asleep. Luckily, for him, he lived through what could've been a multi-fatality accident.

• The year I rode the bus three-days-a-week to school, on a black-ice day, a little ragtop sports car lost control of his vehicle and veered off the highway and down a small decline, flipping end-over-end three times. The bus stopped and another passenger and I carefully avoided other vehicles that hit the slick road surface in order to check whether or not the driver of the wrecked car survived. When we got to where the car rested there was already someone standing and staring at the wreck. I said, "Let's see if we can retrieve the guy in the car." He said, "I am the guy! It's a good thing I had a roll bar installed or I wouldn't be standing here talking to you guys. I'll bet my wife won't rag on me anymore about spending money to have the bar installed."

BUS COMMUTING

In 1981 the cost of gas got so high (probably over $1.50) I decided to ride a commercial bus that made a round trip from Tacoma to Bainbridge Island (about 60+ miles). The morning trip picked me up about 6:30 in Gig Harbor on the highway near where I parked my car, and returned me around 4:30 in the afternoon. I could ride the bus cheaper than driving my car.

Generally, I rode shotgun, just behind the driver, while the other passengers who worked at Naval Submarine Base Bangor, near Poulsbo, dozed. Then one day at the Bangor gate, I was asked to get off the bus while it made its 20-minute run dropping off the government workers. Whoa! Get off a commercial bus and stand in the elements with no shelter for 20-minutes? Hey, I paid to ride the bus, not stand outside.

When I get upset, I write letters.

March 5, 1981
Commanding Officer
Naval Submarine Base, Bangor
Bremerton, Washington

Dear Sir:

Re: Expulsion from commercial bus at Bangor gate

        While commuting from Gig Harbor to Poulsbo

I know you are a busy person and probably have many pressing matters
at hand, but I ask that you spend a few minutes reading this letter and
consider a recent problem that concerns your base.

A few weeks ago I started riding the Cascade Trailways Bus from Gig
Harbor (near my home) to Poulsbo where I have worked as a high school
teacher for the past 14 years. One of the stops before Poulsbo is Bangor,
where everybody but me gets off. Until March 2, two shuttle buses met
the Bangor personnel at the main gate and drove them to their designated
buildings, while I proceeded on to Poulsbo. On March 2, the shuttle
buses ceased running and the Cascade Trailways Bus drove on Base and
deposited the Bangor personnel at their various work places.

Although my time on the bus was lengthened 20 minutes, I didn't mind,
because I could snooze a little while longer. My snooze was abruptly
ended on March 4th at 6:40 when I was forced to get off the bus, wait for
15 minutes in a building (the guard shack), then walk to the highway
and wait another five minutes in the rain because the bus comes out a
different gate than it goes in. There is no safe way to get from the gate to
the highway (Clear Creek Road) and no shoulder or safe place to wait for
the bus, plus getting off a nice dry, warm bus and then standing in the
cold, wet weather isn't that great for one's health.

- I would ask that since I am a paying commuter on a public mode
  of transportation that:

- I be allowed to get a pass to ride through the base on the bus

- Reinstate the shuttle bus

- Bangor provide a weatherproof bus shelter on Clear Creek Road and Luoto Road

- Bangor give me a 40-minute a day job while I wait for the bus

[I gave several reasons why I was not a security risk to their base including the fact that I had a Top Secret security clearance while serving my military tour of duty]

In other words, I am not a threat to your base's security. I just want to ride the bus without the hassle of getting off and on four times a day, plus I am concerned about my safety and comfort.

Our motto at our post in Japan was "Forewarned is Forearmed," and I am giving you first crack at speedily resolving this problem so I don't have to continue up the Chain of Command.

I only ride the bus Tuesdays, Wednesdays and Thursdays until the second week in June.

Thank you for your time in this matter.

Sincerely,

Don Edgers

Suddenly, I was classified as the 'bus driver's assistant' from that time on.

Whenever a substitute driver was put on the route, he was told to ask the 'school teacher' to tell him where the stops were. One time we got a bus that, if it had to stop, would die, and the starter didn't work. There were only four of us as passengers when the bus conked out. Since the starter didn't work, we had to get out and push for a compression start. Fortunately, we were on level ground and we didn't have to push very far before it roared to life with a cloud of Diesel exhaust. Our hands were totally black from pushing the grimy rear-end of our conveyance, but the bus had a restroom with paper towels which cleaned up three of us. The fourth happened to be behind the exhaust pipe and was covered beyond a paper towel cleanup. The next year, the bus route changed, so I returned to commuting by car.

The Hitchhiker

During the course of a yearly 20,000-mile-commute on many rural roads, I saw more than my share of backward-walking people with outstretched arm and thumb pointed to the sky. I had developed a sort of hitchhiker phobia, and made it a point to never pick up roadside ride-begging strangers. My rider-avoidance strategy consisted of not making eye contact by faking that I was fumbling or reaching for something in the car, or glancing at my outside rearview mirror or something on the opposite side of the road. After safely bypassing the perceived intruder, I'd feel a little guilty, but rationalized that a probable near-death encounter with a psycho had been averted.

Sometimes, just the sight of my travel-worn, 1964 VW Bug caused many a hiker to drop their arm and turn their back to discourage me from picking them up. Also, the car didn't have a front passenger seat, making it virtually impossible to offer somebody a ride unless they wanted to sit behind me on the back seat.

Ten miles into my jaunt home one late afternoon, I was traveling a lonely tree-lined stretch of road, when an out-of-place hitcher came into view. I prepared to go into my avoidance strategy at the first sight of a thumb in the air, but this guy had a different technique. He held a hand-lettered cardboard sign with the name of a town 30 miles distant. Suddenly, a wave of compassion overcame my distrust, and I pulled over. Apologizing for the lack of a front seat, I asked him what he was doing hitching on the lightly traveled road. He replied, "I was praying that a Christian would give me a ride. You are a Christian, aren't you?" I had the feeling at this point that I might hear the theme from TV's "Twilight Zone." The question made me apprehensive, but thought that I qualified because of periodic church attendance, and said, yes.

In order to divert him from starting on an evangelical pitch I asked him why he was hitching a ride to such a distant point on a lonely road. He explained that he worked part-time in food service on the naval base near the town of my job, and he couldn't afford to drive to his job, so he hitchhiked. He had worked a few years in a lumber mill as a sawyer, making good money, but had become an alcoholic. It was ruining his marriage and he had a young family of two kids with one on the way. He asked God to deliver him from alcoholism and give him direction in his life. After praying, he said it was just like a weight had been lifted, and he had absolutely no desire to drink for the first time in years. He quit his job that kept him away from his family during the week and set about finding a job closer to home, and the part-time job was the result. Even though the job barely covered food and rent of a single-wide mobile home, he was no longer trusting in himself and the bottle to get him through each day. He was trusting the Lord to be his savior. This admission sent a shiver up my spine.

I dropped him off on the highway near where he lived, with the promise to pick him up the next morning. A couple of days after giving him rides, he asked if I would drive to his home in order to meet his wife who wanted to thank me for being so kind to him. At the mobile home, I was dumbfounded by the sight of his little family and very pregnant wife. They were obviously destitute. The kids didn't have shoes or coats that fit them, his wife had not been to the doctor during her pregnancy and was due in a month or so. Christmas was only weeks away with no presents for anybody!

What really spoke to me about his faith was a discussion we had about tithing. Even though he didn't have much of anything and a part-time minimum-wage job, he gave 10% of take-home pay to his church. "Everything we have is from the Lord, and we as Christians are asked to give back 10% to the church. He delivered me from a life as an alcoholic and got me a job, so I trust Him for daily guidance and provision."

I attended my church the Sunday after my dirt-poor-family encounter and told the hitchhiker's story to the congregation. After the service, practically everybody came to me to offer assistance. Shortly before Christmas, I presented the family with hundreds of dollars in cash, clothing, Christmas presents, a tree and decorations, all donated by my church. His church came up with doctor care, hospital expenses, and he got a decent full-time job. His newfound faith provided him with God's provision and affected me profoundly.

In the remaining years of commuting, I ran through 10 more worn vehicles, and my hitchhiker phobia gradually disappeared. Roads became highways – highways became freeways posted with signs saying "No Hitchhiking."

I became aware of how fortunate I was to have a full-time job, a stick built home, and a car. I also began tithing. All this change in attitude was brought about by taking a chance on picking up a hitchhiker.

~15~

Memorable Colleagues

I like to think that I got along with all my colleagues – some better than others. Since we were in the same occupation to teach those in our classrooms or area of instruction the subject(s) of our particular discipline or specialty, we were a 'mutual admiration society.' I could fill a book with stories of my fellow teachers and administrators, but will have to limit my descriptions to the most memorable.

Principals:

"Leaders establish the vision for the future and set the strategy for getting there; they cause change. They motivate and inspire others to go in the right direction and they, along with everyone else, sacrifice to get there." (John Kotter)

The first principal I worked under was an enigma to me from the beginning. True, he had a number of problems on his hands concerning his high school responsibilities. For the teachers under his wing, especially beginning teachers, there wasn't much to encourage them. That, and the man was critical and demanding under daunting conditions. For example, he'd come into the classroom with the pretense of checking the thermostat, then hang around for a while to see if you were doing your job the way he thought it should be done. Normally, an observation would be scheduled, (per teacher union's contract requirements) with a follow-up session in the principal's office. His 'thermostat checks' were a way around contract guidelines. When he came in for a scheduled observation, his attention span seemed to lag, and if he didn't fall asleep (which actually occurred in my as well as others' classes) he'd leave well before the class ended. Once, he docked me for my dress in a well-worn suit (we had to dress with a jacket and tie through the 1970s), which really upset me, because I wasn't able to afford to buy new or used clothes if I wanted to eat. I learned to darn my socks, and wore my army low quarter shoes until and after the soles had holes.

Another time, when I team-taught a unit to three different sophomore English classes, I was criticized for my teaching techniques and management compared to the other sophomore English teachers. He thought my charges didn't learn as much. It just so happened that all the students had been given a comprehension test to see how much they had learned from the units taught. I asked him which teacher he thought had the best result. He believed the teacher with the most experience would score the highest and I would be the lowest. He was doubtful of my report of the test results that showed my unit was at the top, with his favorite at the bottom. However, he didn't ever bother me about my classroom technique after checking the facts.

I'd been teaching for two months when my 'motivationally-challenged' principal came upon me hurrying to a distant classroom, to harangue me about getting my debate class geared up for competition in the next quarter. I was in the midst of getting my first drama production underway, and my wife was 8 ½ months pregnant, so the comment hit a nerve. I stopped, got in his face, and told him what was going on in my life, and that I was doing the best I could do, and to get off my back!

After teaching for two years, a teacher from another school district joined our faculty and scored a planning period – something I thought I deserved if I survived two years. When I complained, the principal thought I probably deserved study hall supervision as a break from nonstop teaching. When I sent a disruptive student to his office, the student returned with a smile on his face, presented a note from the principal saying I'd have to keep him in study hall because there wasn't any place else to put him. He'd just undermined my authority big time, so I marched the student back to his office, demanding that something be done with the student or I refused to be a study hall teacher, and would trade study hall for the planning period the new teacher had, that I deserved. The student ended up working for the janitor, and my study hall remained under control.

VICE PRINCIPALS

V. P. Lady #1

Miss Ellis, close to my mother's age, was a former shorthand and manual (as in pre electric) typing teacher and business related classes, who because of sheer tenacity and seniority, became the school's vice-principal. Normally a cheery and pleasant looking lady, her stern-sounding and loud voice belied the fact she was less than five feet in height. The kids and staff willingly respected and obeyed her. Her primary weakness was her reluctance to kick out troublesome and sometimes, dangerous students. One afternoon, as I entered the lunchroom, I encountered a crowd gathered around two fighting boys. By the time I go to them, one boy was lying unconscious on the floor. His victor, a large boy, was kicking him in the head with his cowboy boots. I sensed that he was out of control, so kept my distance while trying to convince him that he had killed him. With a glassy-eyed look on his face he responded, "Good!" The attempted murderer happened to be a belligerent bully and non-respecter of authority who needed to be removed from our school. I expressed my concern to both the principal and vice principal with the caveat that if this kid wasn't kicked out of our school, I would quit! The boy was kicked out, and accepted into the army to fight in Viet Nam. I never heard anything else about him.

Miss Ellis retired after 59 years in education and continued substitute teaching well into her eighties, and passed away at the age of 94.

V.P. Lady #2

This little lady, much younger than our previous female administrator, came into our facility like a yellow jacket to a summer picnic. She must have felt like she had to prove herself and impose her perceived authority right off the bat, sort-of like Civil War Admiral David Farragut whose mantra was, "Damn the torpedoes, full speed ahead!"

"A leader is not an administrator who loves to run others, but someone who carries water for his people so that they can get on with their jobs" (Robert Townsend)

Administration wasn't this lady's strong suit, but our school was
contracted with her, so we hoped she'd get with the program and develop
a sense of how we operated in our school-community. This didn't
happen. I had a run-in with her concerning how she thought the Year
Book class should be run, and told me I wasn't following procedures
for running the class. I informed her there weren't procedures because
this was a new class, and I was trying to run it with the least amount of
interruptions to other classes by scheduling picture taking during lunch
periods. This evolved into an argument that was taking up productive
time, so I told her, "Just quit wasting my time, and get the hell out of
here!" This infuriated her and she retorted, "I'm putting this into your
file and you'll regret it." "Fine!" I replied, "Just leave!"

She also picked on other male teachers to the point that one of them
chose to teach in another school, and another to seriously think about
early retirement. Then there was the "untamable" social studies teacher
who refused to listen to her explanation of why she lectured the faculty
about why we couldn't have a Christmas Concert. When she shouted,
"You'll listen anyway!" He departed. She wasn't my supervisor, but I
knew how I would've reacted to her rant – cover my ears, stomp my feet
and yell, "AAAAAAAAAAAH!!!"

I wasn't bothered by her again until the end of the school year when
she was critical of the final product. Because the year book staff and
I had worked so hard to produce a quality product, it was like a slap
to our faces. Upon receiving this awful comment, I walked out of my
classroom, went to the faculty room and told those there to tell the
principal to get someone to cover my classes because I quit! I was
dead serious, too. With just a matter of days left in the school year, I
discovered from others at school that I'd created quite a sensation. I
received calls from the principal, fellow teachers, students, even the
School Board president, urging me to come back. I got an envelope from
school containing petitions and letters urging me to return. I was very
flattered and encouraged by the support of the school's community. The
principal asked me what it would take to sign a contract to teach the next
year, and I told him that I would sign it, but would 'walk' if the 'lady'
was back and continued her tactics to demoralize our school atmosphere.
The 'offender' wasn't rehired and the other vice principal took a job as
a principal in another school district. Their replacements turned out to

be very competent. One of the new vice principals eventually became the principal and was replaced by another man who fit nicely into the school's community. All three administrators ran the school efficiently and effectively for the remainder of my tenure at school.

"Outstanding leaders go out of their way to boost the self-esteem of their personnel. If people believe in themselves, it's amazing what they can accomplish." (Sam Walton)

TEACHERS

English Teachers

Even though I taught subjects outside of English, I was considered to be a member of the English Department, so had most of my close contacts with teachers of this subject.

I have the highest regard for those who choose to teach high school **English** in that these individuals have to be well read, well educated, dedicated, organized, etc., etc., etc. ------. I can't think of a subject that takes as much personal time in knowledge, preparation and paperwork. An English teacher with a 'normal' family life is an oxymoron in my book. Also, if family life, time to do activities and eight-hours of sleep aren't important – teaching English is your cup 'a tea. Except for a couple of these qualifiers, I didn't qualify. I didn't *choose* to teach English and coffee is my choice of beverage.

I only had two sophomore English classes, and they took more time than all the others combined, making it somewhat stressful – at least to the conscientious instructor. An example: There was an unmarried teacher of this subject, who after over 30 years, upon retiring had only three days of sick days she hadn't taken out of 320 she earned. I suspect that most of those 317 'sick' days were used to 'recharge' her batteries.

MARTIN

If I had one teacher to pick as #1, it would be Martin. He was smart, interesting, entertaining, quirky and dedicated.

- **Smart**: Master's Degree, Head of English department, taught English 12 (AP), Latin (advised the Latin Club) and humanities.

- **Interesting**: A bachelor who lived in an inherited house, raised rhododendrons from seed and a good cook.

- **Entertaining**: Feigned the start of ulcers or heart condition and would drag out a bottle of Pepto Bismol® from his mail box, cupboard shelf in the faculty room or a drawer in whatever classroom he was teaching. With everybody watching, he'd give the bottle a good shake, unscrew the cap, take a swig, and exclaim, while returning the bottle to its place, "Good Lord, these kids are going to be the death of me!"

He obtained a shopping cart which he used to move books, papers and supplies from one classroom to another. One Christmas, his 'friends' on the faculty presented him with a tricycle bell, bicycle horn, and rearview mirror for the transport, which he chose not to install.

- **Quirky**: Hated wearing a tie (required in the teacher's dress code for men). He had two ties in his wardrobe: a bow tie which he kept in his mailbox in case he forgot to wear his long knit tie, which shortened throughout the year as it unraveled.

Being a bachelor with rather frugal tastes and a good income because of inheritance, tenure and advanced degree, he kept several past-months' checks in his wallet that he would only cash when all the money drawn from a previous check was gone. The reason I know this is that I was helping him haul manure for his rhododendrons one time, and he promised to take me to dinner at a restaurant as a reward. When he checked his wallet he realized there wouldn't be enough to cover the expense, so he drove to the bank. In his wallet were <u>four</u> uncashed paychecks. He cashed the oldest one, putting the entire amount in his wallet.

Martin wasn't what one would classify as suave, debonair or handsome, but rather pleasantly plain with a mouth on the verge of breaking into a smile. Very popular with his charges, the Latin Club decided to raise money for its coffers by selling calendars with his image as the logo.

The paparazzi of the time (several girls in his classes) took a fancy to him or liked to see how he would react so would try to follow him home. Well, he became paranoid about the situation, so would leave school as late as possible, then drive to a 'fake' destination and make a roundabout trip to his house. If he saw a car following him, he would drive to his house and knock on the door, pretending that he was visiting somebody. If a suspected car remained in the area, he'd leave and visit his sister who lived nearby. If he made it home undetected, he'd park his car out of sight.

A couple of faculty members liked to stir up a reaction to Martin's love life, and would send fake love notes from our elderly librarian, proclaiming her passion for our English department chairman. His mailroom reactions never failed to be priceless.

- **Dedicated**: As a department head, he listened to and worked on our concerns. He didn't back down from 'bullying' from his superiors and they respected his wisdom and logic. His primary concern was for the best education possible for students. Martin worked his way into the library, which he labeled 'media center' and got the materials up-to-date. He was an asset to both faculty and students.

One spring day Martin suffered a heart attack while teaching, and his statement about the students being the 'death of me' almost proved to be prophetic. His father had died of heart problems in his thirties, so the genetic-fear always lurked in mind. When Martin returned to duty, he decided to devote his talents to becoming a librarian at the new junior high school. Four years later, while shopping at a market near his home, he had a fatal heart attack.

HOPE

After Martin left the high school, Hope became the head of our English department. She was a dedicated English and journalism teacher. As the years went by, she made me realize English teachers were definitely a different breed of cat.

Hope was an interesting lady. She had a 'gimpy' arm that was virtually useless, yet she didn't let this infirmity slow her down. She wore a wig in the classroom throughout her entire career, because she didn't have time to mess with hair appointments, etc. She chopped her hair with kitchen scissors and went wigless at home. The classroom wigs were different shades of brown and depending on how big of a rush she was in in the mornings, determined the set of her hair. Some days it was close to her eyebrows, other days it set back, and there were 'crooked days,' too. Hair wasn't important to her.

Her 'moods' were somewhat unpredictable, and if one were on her 'list' on a day of wrath, watch out, or look for the nearest rock to crawl under. Yet she could also laugh at herself – like the day she was giving an assignment while standing at the front of class and the elastic on her panties broke, dropping them to the floor. She said that only one student saw them, so got the "look of death" from Hope, who managed to kick them over to her desk. When the students were working on their assignment, the wayward undergarment was picked up and deposited in a desk drawer. When the janitor emptied the wastebasket after school that day he probably wondered why clean panties were included with the other waste.

She had no family to support, so much of her paycheck went to hobbies and collections. One of her collections was mugs and steins. They filled several cabinets and shelves. One bedroom in her rented three-bedroom house contained a model train setup with miles of tracks, lots of scenery, figures and accessories. The pricey collection had uncountable cars and engines.

Video recorders/players in their early days came in two formats, Beta and VHS. Hope chose Beta, and bought many expensive prerecorded tapes.

She was also a devout baseball fan with an almost adoration for the Seattle Mariners. You can imagine her ecstasy when one of her high school students became a major league baseball player, eventually playing for the Seattle Mariners.

Hope lived less than ten minutes away from school, and she didn't venture far from our little community, so her cars had minimum mileage on them. Those of us who went through cars like monkeys in a banana tree, waited with bated breath for the mention that she 'might' get a new car, almost begging for the right of first refusal to buy her car. But it just so happened she had been advised that she was the owner of a classic Ford Mustang, the price of which was out of range of teachers.

Almost every summer she would take a group of students for a month of travel and study to a foreign country. It was difficult to find a country she hadn't visited. The kids and their parents loved her for taking on this challenge. One summer our daughter went on one of her trips to England, France, Luxembourg, Germany, Yugoslavia, Austria and Italy with a short cruise in the Mediterranean Sea on a Greek cruise ship.

SHARON

I can't imagine reading everything by or about Charles Dickens (my guy is John Steinbeck) but Sharron earned her Masters with Mr. D. as her thesis subject.

This English teacher was in the top-tier of competent teachers. She knew her stuff and challenged students to perform at high levels. Students who were serious about advancing their English knowledge and skills made an effort to get into her classes, and if they made it through her Advanced Placement English classes in good shape, were so prepared, they could skip the required college freshman English classes when they challenged the classes.

Throughout the school year she expertly directed theatrical productions, and in the spring of each year she read compositions for the National Merit Scholarship Program. As the English department chairperson she served us well.

TOM D.

Tom was another high-caliber English teachers who was respected by the faculty and students because of his ability to reach his students in a way that they knew they were receiving important life-long skills. He was serious in his demeanor and behaved like a Christian man.

One spring his 16-year-old daughter attended a Christian conference where she got on the back of a motorcycle for a quick ride, and was killed when the cycle went out of control. The entire faculty was sorely affected, and when we had a meeting, Tom stood up and faced us to tell us how he coped with his daughter's death. I don't believe any one of us could've held up the way he did, as most of us were in tears. He calmly said the only way he could hold up was because of his Christian faith and everything happens for a reason, and he knew he'd see his daughter again in heaven.

I also liked Tom as a friend and colleague. Whenever I spoke at faculty get-togethers he'd comment to me, "I love to hear you speak because you never fail to crack me up." How can you not like someone like that?

JOHN D.

John had a Master's Degree in *poetry*! Ye gads, I can't imagine! He also was a high school classmate with Bill Gates at Lakeside School in Seattle. Creative, he produced a quality literary magazine as well as creative writers and poets.

One year a high number of students signed up to take speech, and as my schedule only allowed me to teach one speech class, the overload class was assigned to John. Never having to take a speech class, he quickly spent extra time with me instructing him and giving him all the handouts I had for my class. He was a good student and was able to intelligently fake his way through the class and actually enjoy it.

Other Subject Teachers

JOHN T.H.

At a distance one wouldn't guess that this stooped swarthy individual was idolized by a majority of the senior class who had to take his class (World Problems). He was a self-confidant, charismatic *social studies* teacher who made his classroom-brood work for him. They seemed to want his approval because of his personality and reputation. Administrators weren't always enamored by his persona and periodically tried to 'tame' him, to no avail.

He also appealed to those approaching driving age, as a driver's education teacher. The other driving instructors tended to get "up-tight" with a car full of nervously-sweating fledglings and used the passenger side brake pedal so often the cars had to have the brakes redone before getting a newer model car.

With several years of teaching drivers education behind him, John understood the minds of new drivers and would demonstrate to the faculty in the teachers' lounge and exaggerate what they might do when they hit the road. In the faculty room we enjoyed his descriptive experiences. If one of his charges was mentioned as particularly lacking in ability, and we weren't aware of the student, he'd send the student to our classroom with a note saying, "This is the one." We'd tell the student to tell the sender of the message, "O.K."

A Mathematics Teacher

~*~

I respect teachers of *mathematics* and their ability to explain to the mathematically challenged how to make sense of how using numbers in logical prescribed ways works, and explain why it matters.

One of our teachers in the math department who began teaching in 1950 was "one for the books." A late middle-aged bachelor of ordinary looks, he took on a yellowish cast to skin and clothes due to the overuse of the chalkboard, chalk and erasers in the explanation of his discipline. Unfortunately, those not choosing to improve their skills were unrelenting in their disrespect for their teacher and fellow students. The distractions ranged from pennies being pitched to the front of the room while his back was to the class, to a dead duck thrown into the classroom by a disrupter passing by in the hallway.

He seemed to spend 30 years in classroom hell because he didn't have a personality suited to dealing with squirrelly high school students forced to take a required course.

DUANNE

The calmest teacher in our school, started teaching in our building the same year I did, and had two or three years teaching experience in another school district. As a *business and typing* teacher he was able to maintain his cool, even when a kid threw up in one of the typewriters.

His students were amazed at his calm demeanor and wondered if something was wrong with him. So, I informed some students that he had a bad heart, and if he got excited he might have a heart attack. This became a rumor that lasted for several years, and served him well as I don't think he had any discipline problems. Although, he *did* have a heart attack at home that his wife had to attend to and apply CPR. When he returned to classroom duty, the rumor became reality and the kids never gave him any guff.

CLAYTON

A ten-year U.S. Marine Corps veteran, this **biology** teacher was a stickler for discipline, and if one happened to be in the hallways during class time, the sight of a student carrying a chair held to his posterior might be observed. He also had male students do 25-50 pushups. I don't know how misbehaving girls were disciplined – maybe they didn't dare misbehave. According to his students he was well respected and a good teacher.

One year he was chosen by the senior class to be a speaker at graduation. His speech went something like, "I didn't graduate high school, (drafted?) so let's get crackin'!" The kids' loved it.

JOE G.

An ***Industrial Arts*** teacher that needs mention is this teacher, primarily known as the Ag. (Agriculture) teacher, who had started teaching in the district since *1940* when I was one-year-old!

PATTY

This ***science*** teacher was memorable to me because of her inability to eat her lunch in the allotted 25 minutes. The queen of slow chewers, I suspected that she burned more calories chewing than she took in from the food she swallowed. Her slight frame seemed to indicate that this was the case.

She asked me to mentor her in speaking to the faculty at our meetings when she had to make a presentation. My perceived ability to give lighthearted reports appealed to her, so she'd ask for my response to overhead projections she might use and did a good job.

HARRY

Harry was the ***woodshop*** aka industrial arts or carpentry instructor who also drove one of the school buses and volunteered as an EMT for the community's ambulance. Because my metabolism caused me to have a voracious lunchtime appetite, I was conscious of seeing what other faculty members had tucked in their sacks or containers. I come from a fast-eating family – my father being the fastest – so I was able to put away copious amounts of food of various types, while noting that Harry ate the same thing *every* day: bologna sandwich on white bread, a whole dill pickle and a Ding Dong®.

He was the last teacher who was allowed to drive a school bus in order to supplement his pay, and he enjoyed driving the community's ambulance.

The summer of 1968 while he was playing golf with one of the school's football coaches, the coach suffered a heart attack. Harry immediately gave him CPR until the ambulance came, but the coach didn't survive.

The carpentry class built several 8' X 10' fiberglass greenhouses for $150 and I bought three of them for me, my brother-in-law and a neighbor. While bringing them to Fox Island, a state trooper pulled me over to find out where they came from, because he wanted to buy one. Oh, and one of my brake lights didn't work!

JOHN C.

One teacher who was the epitome of an exemplary teacher was the high school's *music* teacher. His ability to direct both vocal and instrumental musicians was almost incomprehensible. His students performed in concerts, assemblies, parades, athletic events, musical plays and any other venue requiring music. From the 1968 *Viking* Year Book there are pictures of 50 students in *Band*, 42 in *Orchestra*, 49 in *Choir*, 69 in *Chorus*, plus lesser numbers in *Stage Band* and a girls' singing group called *the Northern Lights*. The only group not in uniform or dressed up was Chorus. I asked him how he managed to handle so many events and students without going crazy, and he replied, "I seem to operate better when I'm under pressure – and what makes you think I'm not crazy?"

JOHN M.

The primary *art* teacher during my time at the high school, was the most talented art teacher in a variety of art forms imaginable. His artwork and those of his gifted students graced various areas of the school building. A very large Viking-themed mosaic-tiled piece covered an outdoor wall of the music building. Paintings he did of the faculty were displayed in the faculty lounge along with an almost life-size papier- mâché statue painted to look like a bronze sculpture. His designs were used by the school district on their stationary, and his designs were used by various school programs. It was like having a Michal Angelo on the staff of our high school. Virtually, the whole school district appreciated his artistic abilities. His students were very fortunate to have had John as an instructor.

Special Education Teachers – I have a great admiration for those who have chosen this area of instruction. The majority of these special students have mental (psychological, retardation) or physical limitations that preclude them from attending traditional classes. The Special Ed. teachers are usually assisted by adult teacher aides who also have to have training, understanding, appreciation and patience for those under their care. In other words, Special Education teachers and their assistants are a *special* breed of educators.

BRIAN

Ordinarily, teachers who just can't survive on teachers' pay, leave teaching to make a living in another occupation. This was not so with a potentially wealthy man who sold out his partnership in what turned out to be a popular boat building company. The straw that broke the camel's back happened on a busy highway while transporting some boats to a customer and losing part of his load. He decided to return to school to become a *special education* teacher and demonstrated a knack for reaching and teaching these students.

STEVE N.

Steve was a multitalented middle-aged man who taught *biology, coached* tennis and became the *athletic director*. As athletic director his office was in the MAX (Media. Athletics. Xerox) Building, so I had daily contact with him when he performed his athletic scheduling. When he wasn't in his office, he had a loud answering machine with a greeting performed in gruff gangster-like voice demanding callers to leave a message. The answering machine voice could sometimes be heard in my classroom across the hall from his office to the delight of the students in my classroom. On occasion, I might have to go to his classroom in the main building. In his room was a free-range (except at night) ferret for student enjoyment? All who entered the room were aware that the critter was somewhere on the premises, even if they couldn't see it. If the creature showed up, Steve would keep it at bay so that it wouldn't run up a pant leg. But if it happened to go up your pants, the tennis coach had a tennis racquet handy in order to whack it.

JIM H.

Jim was a basketball *coach, teacher* and *counselor* who, after teaching and coaching at a private high school for nine years and coaching at UPS, came to our school where he taught English, mathematics and eventually became a counselor. He had played college ball for Seattle University along with basketball legend Elgin Baylor and was on the Seattle University team that came in 2nd in the nation at the 1958 NCAA basketball championship tournament. He was able to put his experience as a basketball coach into practice at our high school, producing some outstanding players. In 2016 he works as an assistant coach at the high school.

A Social Studies Teacher

~ * ~

An 'unusual', small-statured, banty rooster-type (lively) individual was a popular *social studies* teacher for the reasons he made his subject interesting and somewhat unpredictable in its presentation to his students. You might say he taught outside of the box. Personally, I thought he was a good teacher who went out of his way to stimulate and educate his students.

He had a particular fascination with the Viet Nam War, and claimed to be a veteran of that conflict. Because of this he wanted to do a unit of study in his classes, featuring some commercial films that portrayed the violence and life and death struggles involved. The problem was these films were rated R. This drew attention of parents and even a newspaper columnist who strongly objected. In his defense of his request he said something like, "The students needed to see what it was like for soldiers like me who experienced this event." The newspaper columnist did some digging into the teacher's U.S. Army record, and discovered he never served in active duty. With this fact revealed, he disappeared from the school district, leaving many students and teachers sorely disappointed in how they'd been hoodwinked over the years. He was a very effective teacher, though. I noticed an odd thing he did in the faculty room. When he brought fruit for lunch, he'd peel off the sticker from the skin and place it on woodwork near the coat racks. In a year's time there were many stickers accumulated, which had to be removed during the summer by the custodians.

JIM R.

Jim was a *social studies* teacher who decided to leave teaching in order to become a lawyer. He went to Southern California to study and while there managed to get on some popular TV quiz shows: *21*, and *Hollywood Squares*. Classrooms having TV sets tuned in to watch his daytime performances. He did extremely well, winning several cars, trips, cash, etc. He became a lawyer and then a judge in our county in later years.

SPEKEN? – HABLE? – PARLEZ? (Foreign Language) TEACHERS

All the teachers of foreign languages seemed to have had a livelier style of presentation than teachers of other disciplines. Each language had celebrations, festivals, etc. that got the students into the spirit of the country of whose language they were studying. One Spanish class went to Mexico during Eastertime, and the teacher came close to dying and had to be resuscitated after drowning. One of the French teachers taught nearly 40 years. All of the teachers in this subject were wonderful colleagues and added greatly to our faculty and the lives of the students they taught.

~16~

Memorable Students

Most student who attended the high school where I taught or had me as a teacher (thousands) probably want to be remembered for one reason or another (good or bad). The fact is, most students, even though they were great kids, just don't make the cut. If I were to make my teacher tales a movie title, it would be *The Good (10%), the Bad (5%), the Interesting (10%) and the Normal (75%)*.

During the 1970s when Viet Nam was being inhabited by some of our former high school students, I would be visited by 'secret agents' to ask me about certain students I had taught, who were seeking a security clearance. In one case the 'agent' asked about a girl I'd had the previous year. Try as I might, even after looking at her photo in a Yearbook, I drew an absolute blank.

Bigboy – This student was memorable because he was the heaviest student I had in my first year of teaching. Nobody seemed to hang around with him much, possibly because of his weight and grating-type personality. Also, he was not picked on, because of his size. His apparent lack of friends told the tale of a disgruntled overweight kid.

We had a 20-minute period, called X-period, where students had to go somewhere for club meetings, tutoring or to just hang out. "Bigboy", without fail, would hang out with the kids in the drama greenroom and where my office occupied one of the two changing rooms. He'd invariably get in my face and disrespectfully call me 'Doon.' After telling him not to do this, and very close to the time my wife was due to have a baby, he called me 'the name.' I gruffly told him to not call me by that name. Whereupon, he challenged me with, "Or if I do, what are you going to do about it – Doon?" The door to my office was open, so I quickly went for him and pushed his bulky body into the space, causing him to fall onto his back. I slammed shut the door and leaped upon his stomach and cocked my fist, saying, "If you ever call me that again, or show disrespect to me, I'll beat the crap out of you! Understand?

By this time, the students in the greenroom were knocking on the door and asking if I was okay. Still astride my student adversary, I answered, "We're fine."

My flat-on-his-back adversary was red-faced and shocked by my sudden move, but gained newfound respect for my position and situation. He never bothered me again, and word must've spread about my encounter, because more members of the student body waved and said hi to me in the halls. Various faculty members also made enquiries about the "rumored encounter." Evidentially I tamed a bull in the China closet.

Two years after the greenroom encounter, I had a student approach me and say, "Hi, Mr. E, how's it goin'?" I didn't recognize him, so asked who he was. It was Bigboy less half his body weight! He explained how the army made him lose many pounds. He shaped up quite well.

Gentle Giant – This student. At about 6'4", weighed in at about 325 and wrestled in the unlimited weight class. I got to know him because of drama and play productions, and would sometimes drive him home after play rehearsals. There were some old non-functional cars parked in the yard of his house located in the boonies. A couple of times the giant would ask permission to sleep overnight on the couch in the storage space under the stage. When I asked why, he'd explain that his dad was on a bender and would beat him up and make him spend the night in one of the derelict vehicles at his house, and it was getting too cold to sleep there. I'd seen his father at a wrestling match, and it was obvious that the father would be no match for the giant son. I said that I was surprised his father could beat him up. It was explained that if he didn't let his dad beat him up, then his dad would take it out on his mom. I almost cried at the situation, but didn't know what I could do about it.

Brian J. – Brian came to my class in a well-used, battery-powered wheelchair and accompanied by an aide. He was unable to lift or move his hand more than a few inches, and it was painful for him to move his head. He spoke in a very soft voice. My Film Study class was the only class he took outside of Special Education (because of his physical limitations) during his time in school. I had his older sister in a previous class, and she explained her brother's situation and wondered if it would be possible for him to take a class from me. I didn't see why not, so the die was cast.

Most of the lessons in this class required the students to complete a written assignment or test. Brian could have had his aide do the report. With great painful effort the handicapped boy did all the assignments which required the aide to move the paper sort of like a typewriter.

After he graduated, Brian went to a nursing home. I received a request to come to the home for a visit, and we had an enjoyable conversation, mostly about the Seattle Seahawks. Some of the players had visited him and left autographed pictures to this avid fan. Not long after my visit, Brian passed away. I went to his memorial and spoke about our friendship and his gumption.

Gail A. – Physically, Gail at the age of 18, was perhaps the size of a 13-year-old. He had blond hair, blue eyes, was friendly looking and had an asthmatic-sounding voice. For a kid with cystic fibrosis he didn't play on anybody's sympathy, and displayed a wonderful sense of humor: He drove a full-size car, and sat on a cushion in order to see over the dash board. Once, when he stopped at a gas station, the teen-aged attendant asked him how old he was, to which he said, "13."

"Well, what are you doing driving a car?"

"My parents are away, and I need to get groceries, so I 'borrowed' it."

The attendant thought this was so funny that he went into the station office, pointing to "the 13-year-old", and laughing hysterically.

Gail had to go to the hospital periodically to get his lungs cleared and sometimes had a prolonged stay. During one of his hospital stays, the student body printed T-shirts with his picture on it. When he came back to school, there was a special assembly where everyone wore their shirts and the principal declared a Gail Anderson Day. He was genuinely admired by students and teachers. About two years after graduation he succumbed to his affliction – age 20.

Girls with drug habits - Another memorable student, in that she had a drug habit which started in her preteen days, explained to me how she developed the problem. She lived next to a sports equipment magnet who smuggled drugs in imported water skis. He shared some of his drugs with his little neighbor who developed a drug habit. A few years later I received a note of appreciation for treating her nicely and not berating her for being on drugs. She had been successfully rehabilitated and drug-free for years.

Another girl came to a faculty meeting one year to tell her tales of being hooked on cocaine, angel dust, and other up-the-nose drugs. She told of daily taking drugs at school, using a doctor's note that said she had a bladder problem and should be excused from classes to use the restroom when necessary. Her classroom performance, absences and personal demeanor was suspicious because she had been doing well until partway into her senior year. I was suspicious of her doctor's note, and whenever she used it with me, I would comment that as long as she used it for its intended purpose, and did not use it to take drugs, it was okay. She mentioned at our meeting that I was the only teacher who commented on her suspected drug use. Her message to us was, "If a student's performance, attendance and appearance show signs of neglect, set up a meeting with the student's parents and counselors to find out why. One faculty member asked the girl why she just didn't quit? The girl's reply was, "The next time you have diarrhea, just tell yourself that you just don't have to use a toilet!"

Anxious Recluse – A freshman boy was introduced to me by one of the counselors who said he had a student that was very reclusive, but very interested in filmmaking and thought that maybe I could get this boy off to a better start in high school because he was in Special Education classes at this time. I agreed to meet with this student in my classroom during my 25-minute lunch period so that I could talk to him about his hobby. He told me a little about himself and that the reason he was in Special Education classes was that he couldn't stand to be in classes, in the hallways or where there were lots of the people. I agreed to let him bring some of his films to my room during my lunch time so I could look at them and discuss filmmaking with him. After viewing his films, I realized he had a talent that he could take advantage of, especially in my film classes where we made films. He said that he would try to take a class from me but he didn't know if he'd be able to succeed because of his anxiousness of being around lots of people. I told him that if he felt overwhelmed that he could just go into my back office, which had an outside door, and he could tell me that he was going "to see the counselor." Agreeing to these terms, he enrolled in a Media Now class where we were doing films. The assignment that I gave the class was on splicing films and threading projectors and things related to movies. These are all things that were familiar to him and which he had performed many times. As soon as I gave this assignment he said, "I need to see the counselor." I met him in my office to see what the problem might be. He said that he was afraid he'd screw up and I explained to him that he had done all of these things before successfully and there was nothing to worry about. He said he was afraid that he would make a mistake and that everyone would laugh at him. I explained to him that nobody had ever laughed at anybody in my classes for making a mistake, and even if they did what difference did it make? From that point on he did just fine in the class and ended up being sort of looked up to because of his abilities and skills in editing films.

At the end of the year I would present trophies that people had donated to me over the years for various sports or activities to students who had shown creativity in their films that they had made throughout the year. The Special Education boy had earned awards because of his skills in filmmaking. I told him that I would present them at an awards assembly and would he accept an award at the assembly? He explained to me that he was still very nervous about being around crowds and an assembly was something he'd never attended, so, he would not accept the award at the assembly. The next year the same situation came about at the end of the year, and again he was going to receive a film trophy. This time he said. I'll think about it, but don't count on it. His senior year he had become much more confident and again when I offered the awards, he said he thought he *might* come up on stage to accept the award, but not to count on it. Surprise, surprise! He came up and receive the award, and appeared in front of a crowd for the first time in his life. This same year I was chosen to be the commencement speaker and in my speech I said I hadn't had time to prepare much for the speech so I was going to pick somebody from the senior class to help give it. Of course I was just joking. However, the talented filmmaker told me after this speech that he thought I was speaking directly to him and he was thinking about what he was going to say.

Effective Dyslectic – A highly affective dyslectic boy joined my Media
Now class whom I found to be very interesting from the first time I
ever saw him. He had a pleasant face and related well to his peers, who
admired him because he didn't consider himself special in any particular
way and had a wonderful personality. But special he was! This boy had
extreme dyslexia. Numbers in particular were nonexistent in his brain.
For example, one summer he went on a bicycle trip from Washington
State to Washington, DC with another boy. When I asked him how long
it took him to make the trip. His response was, "a *long* time!" When I
asked him how many days it took, he said he didn't know how many
days.

We did an exercise in my class in photography where the timing for how
long the photo materials needed to be in the different chemicals. The
timing was critical. Knowing his trouble with numbers, I asked him
how he would be able to read the clock. He told me that he looked at an
angle or some unique feature of the number he was supposed to be able
to read. His film and photographs always turned out perfect. In drivers
training the instructor had to spend extra time getting him to be able to
transfer the numbers on the signs to the numbers on the speedometer.
He managed to pass the written and driving tests with flying colors
and got his Washington State Drivers License. During his senior year
he was voted, during homecoming season, as the Homecoming King!
Obviously his classmates thought he was someone who deserved special
recognition. Ten years after graduating, while I was having coffee at a
local mall, up comes this special individual with his wife. They had been
married several years and were enjoying each other's company and the
lives they lived.

Butterfly – I don't remember the name of this girl that was called by
this moniker, but I recall the counselor who assign her to my class
saying, "You are going to have quite an experience with this girl." At
the beginning of her first day in my class, this quickly became obvious.
After she was in her seat, somebody passed by her and said the word
'butterfly,' whereupon she instantly jumped up screaming, "Don't call
me that!" She explained to me that the kids said that to her in order to get
her all riled up. I was reminded of the boy in my fifth grade class who
we drove nuts by saying, "We're gonna getcha!" So I informed the class

that if anybody else chose to call her butterfly they would be kicked out of my class. The rest of the semester passed smoothly.

Little Person - I had a little person in my speech class one year who wasn't able to be seen from the back of the room unless she was standing on a small platform. Her father was a little person, her mother was average size as was her brother. She told the speech class what it was like to be a little person, which was very interesting to all of us. She even spoke about going to a Little Person's Convention in a different state. Because she didn't seem to have many close friends and felt left out of many student activities, she had a desire to get involved in student government. She was a pretty good speaker, so I encouraged her to run for a student office where she would have to speak in front of the entire school. She went through with it and nobody laughed at her, but she didn't get elected. Three or four years after she graduated, she ended up taking her life and her parents called me to ask if I would relate some positive words that could be spoken at her memorial.

Tall – A boy who, at 7'2", told our speech class the handicaps of being so tall. He was unable to buy any shoes from a normal shoe store, cloths from a normal clothing store and couldn't walk into any classroom door without ducking his head. He also had to sit in the front row of every class that he took because his legs were too long to get underneath a normal school desk. One day as I followed him into the main office, I understood his frustration at being so tall. Without exception, every student or faculty member who passed him commented on his height. Fortunately, he was a very good basketball player.

Aaron Sele – I'm going to use this former student's full name because those interested in professional sports will probably recognize this major league pitcher's name. He had a 13-year career with the Red Sox, Rangers, Mariners, Angels, Dodgers and Mets.

His mother was a secretary at our school, so whenever his team was in Seattle he'd stop by the school to see his mom and his baseball coach. I happened to catch him in the office on a hometown game day, and asked him if he'd come to my room, knock on the door and ask for a certain student by name. The unsuspecting student was an ardent Mariners fan and idolized Aaron. When I opened the door to reveal the 6'5" Sele, he asked in a deep voice if he could speak to the student. The student turned the same color as his hair – red, and probably was on the verge of a heart attack, but managed to make his way to the door and into the hall for a brief-memorable-conversation with his hero. I don't know how many major league stars would take the time to do such a mission, but Aaron did.

Thieves – I had many experiences of thievery throughout my school years and even before.

I got caught stealing cookies from a store near our home at about age four. My folks had an account at the store, and I'd charge stuff like Popsicles or gum with no problem, but cookies were not allowed because my dentist and nutrition-conscious father thought I'd consume too many wasted calories and refined flour at one sitting, since I would consume an entire package.* Our next door neighbor in Seattle, when she was home, would supply me with cookies on demand, so I developed a cookie-craving-habit that wasn't supplied at my house. One day, when she wasn't home, I wandered to other houses to see if I could score a cookie or two – or even a Graham cracker. After striking out at houses in my neighborhood, I wandered into new territory and finally found a kind lady who supplied my craving – along with calling the cops on me. It just so happened that Mom was concerned about my hour-long absence and filed an APB with the police. I got a ride home in a police car to be delivered into the arms of my concerned mother. You would think my folks would at least buy me some crackers, but no, I had to steal to feed my habit.

*After being caught with cookie crumbs on my mouth, I pretty much got scared straight.

I tended to trust most students, unless I got a prior warning from others to be careful.

I'm not exactly sure of the motivation for other thieves to steal, but I saw others of this ilk from the time I was a juvenile, throughout my school years, in the army and beyond. Maybe the comedian Flip Wilson was right when he said, as the character, Geraldine, "The Devil made me do it!"

Besides losing money, I had cameras, prerecorded video tapes, posters - like "Just because you're paranoid doesn't mean the whole world's not out to get you!" [It was stolen two times], movie posters, calculators, equipment /supplies, etc. I even had a teacher's assistant steal junk food (cookies or chips) out of my lunch sack. I could understand the cookies, but the potato chips?! The most blatant and mystifyingly-stupid theft was committed by a boy who worked in the library and had charge of our one-and-only reel-to-reel VHS video recorder and video camera. One day he came into my room, and took the equipment, saying, "The library needs it." Other than the athletic department, I used the equipment more than any other teacher. When the athletic department came to my room to use it in order to record a game, I sent them to the library. It wasn't there, and no one else had used it in the meantime. 'Library boy', after concocting a cock & bull story, fessed up that he'd decided to take it home! A few weeks later, after a weekend, the video equipment was stolen from my classroom. It was discovered abandoned in an athletic field. It's surmised that the thief left it because of its bulk or he thought somebody saw him.

Body Odor (B.O.) Boy – One student that was picked-on had a noticeable odor problem, which got so bad that when he came into the room, students would spray room deodorizer in his vicinity. A couple of students approached me about the smell and asked if I could do something about it.

I asked the odiferous student to come into my office where I told him that some classmates were complaining about his odor. Just as a one-eyed person knows he has only one eye, "B.O. Boy" knew that he reeked, but couldn't seem to do anything about it. He showered every day at school, and changed his clothes which he claimed were washed regularly. He thought that his clothes smelled because his two older brothers wore the same clothes years before he got them. Also, his folks couldn't afford to buy him clothes. I referred the situation to a counselor who referred it to the Home Economics' teacher, who got him new clothes, which completely solved the smell situation in the boy's classes.

Autistic Boy who came back on Fridays – My Film Study classes were classes where Special Education (SE) students could be included with other students and not feel intimidated or like outcasts. It was also about the only class where other students could get to see and mix with those in SE. Each Special Education student was accompanied by an aide, and sometimes I would have up to three SE students in a class. I had a SE teacher who told me that the nonverbal student who never spoke in any classes, for some reason would answer, "Here!" when I called his name in my class. Apparently this boy liked me or my class so much that when he was no longer in the class, on Fridays he would come in one door of my classroom, walk between me and the class I was teaching, while carrying a wastebasket, and go out a door on the opposite side of the room. He looked straight ahead as if everyone was invisible. I'd always verbally recognize him and tell him to have a good weekend. My class was always amused, but also looked forward to the ritual.

~17~

Financial Situation

Until I went into the Army, I never had to think about money. I was dependent on my parents. Even though I didn't think much about earning a living, I still liked to engage in activities that paid off some way or another, if not monetarily, in satisfaction and a sense of accomplishment. In Cub Scouts and Boy Scouts the payoff was in Merit Badges. In school we received certificates or (in my case) free lunches. Outside activities, like sports awarded certificates or badges or trophies. The first outside job that paid me in money was as a paperboy for delivery of 75 copies of a local weekly newspaper - $4.00.

At a faculty meeting in the late 1960s, a financial planner who sold (403-B) Tax Sheltered Annuities made the comment, "Even if you can only afford to invest $25.00 a month you will be building up a retirement fund." I thought to myself, '$25.00 a month?! I'll probably be an old man before that happens.' I chose to teach as a career for the satisfaction of doing something I thought I was designed to do and not for the financial payoff. There were many times when, if I wanted to improve my finances, I had to seek out job opportunities I thought I could handle.

Some of the ways I augmented my teacher salary

- Sold shoes from catalogues from Mason®, Bronson® and Hanover® Shoe Companies

- Bus driver/field supervisor for a large berry farm (three summers)

- Delivered films to all the schools in the school district

- Taught night school classes for local community college

- Taught an extension class at the Women's Correction Center

155

- Video Business (videographer) inventory for insurance, weddings, graduations, memorials, job/school applications, wills

- Cherry picker for a large orchard. I was the lone Caucasian and the second-best picker

- Taught classes to teachers for Antioch University/The Heritage Institute and Seattle Pacific University

- Coordinator and teacher of Japanese exchange students for the Pacific American Institute

- Manual laborer for a stump removal company

In the summertime it helped that our food budget was greatly reduced because I grew a large vegetable garden. I was grateful to my father for the example he set for me as a child by growing a Victory Garden in the city and a vegetable garden in the country. We also had many fruit and nut trees as well as grapes and berries. Eventually, as I advanced on the Salary Schedule, I didn't have to seek out methods to bring in more money other than continue taking classes at night and summer school in order to obtain a Master's Degree. By the time I retired, after 28 years of public school teaching, I had increased my income by $40,000 and I had maxed out on the Salary Schedule for years of service and education credits, or from BA + 15 Step 3 to MA + 90 Step 15 This was well beyond my expectations when I first started teaching.

~18~

At the Finish Line

In the spring of the year before I planned to retire (1994) I had to notify the principal that I was going to turn in my resignation at the end of the semester in 1995*.

To Whom It May Concern:

This is to inform you that it is my intention to retire as a classroom teacher at the high school in the North Kitsap School district as of **February 1, <u>1995</u>**.

I have made the decision to terminate my employment for the following reasons:

- I will have commuted from Fox Island to Poulsbo for a total of 445,000 miles by February 1st, and my 1951 Chevrolet can't take it much more. (Actually, I've driven 21 different vehicles, one of which was a 1951 Chevy)

- All of the above mentioned miles took almost 10,000 hours to drive, and now, after nearly 27 years of commuting, I sometimes lose track of where I'm going and end up in places like Olympia and Port Angeles, which really upsets my wife.

- I'm approaching the "magic age" of 55.

- I would like to devote more time to writing, and less time at auto stores, mechanic shops and gas stations.

- My retirement will allow room for a newcomer or two to begin a career in classroom teaching, or free up some money for the North Kitsap School District.

- I will be able to teach Media Now, Film Study and Success for two more quarters, which will be the last time these classes will ever be taught at the high school.

Lest there be any doubt: the North Kitsap School District got more than its money's worth from me in my 38,600 hours in the classroom, and I have done my best to represent North Kitsap in a favorable way.

I wish to express my thanks to the N.K.S.D for hiring me and allowing me to develop new classes and teaching methods. I have enjoyed my teaching career and appreciate receiving pay for something I loved doing.

Sincerely,
Don Edgers

---

*This request was not accepted by the principal due to the havoc it would cause in scheduling and procuring a teacher to replace me for half of a year. I relented, and finished out the 1994-95 school year. The letter above, was read at a School District meeting at the end of school. And I was allowed to be released to my Fox Island neighborhood.

PART III

AS A PRIVATE SCHOOL TEACHER

~19~

Two Years as a Private School Teacher

[1995-1997]

After 28 years of teaching in a Public School, in 1995, I looked forward to sleeping-in, relaxing, puttering around and not having to participate in the daily grind of commuting and performing teaching duties — that is until I ran into a teacher/administrator friend from another school district, and suddenly the proverb "The best laid plans of mice and men often go awry" applied itself to my situation.

This friend retired from public schools the year before and took a job at a Christian school attached to a megachurch that had recently expanded their program from K-8 to 9-12. He had just finished teaching English in the newly opened high school section of the school and he was going to become the school's vice principal. He suggested that I apply to teach at the school because they needed to replace him as the only English teacher. The high school's program had just started there with very few students, and teaching there would be "a piece of cake." After talking this over with my wife, she thought it would be a good plan to keep me constructively occupied rather than a free-range retiree. I was a bit apprehensive because I hadn't taught English for 13 years, and I knew English is a subject that takes a lot of time and energy. However, with a small number of student, perhaps I wouldn't be overwhelmed.

I filled out an application and was called in for an interview with the school's headmaster and principals of the elementary and junior high school. Since I was an "outsider" (non-church member) I needed to be interviewed by the church's senior pastor (similar to a district superintendent in public schools). I passed his inspection and was contracted to teach English, speech and drama for six classes during a seven period day – a radical change from my former school's four-period day and teaching three periods. My salary would be about 2/3 of that of my public school's pay, but I now received retirement from my public school teaching, and my commute distance would significantly

161

cut. Another positive was that the building housing the high school was new. This would be the first time in my teaching career to teach in a new facility.

New Experiences:

I thought I had taught every school schedule possible. We had quarter, trimesters and semesters, usually with six periods in a day. More recently, my public school had been on a four-period schedule to match more closely a collegiate time schedule. The Christian school was operating on a seven period day which to me was jamming a little bit of information into very short time schedule. It seemed like I would take roll, recap the previous day's lesson, give a bit of information and class was over. More time was required for homework than for classwork. It was like waiting in a lunch line to get served, and the lunch period was over before you could eat.

A dress code for students reminded me of the early days (1960s) when a strict code was required for males and females. In public school the code had almost become extinct, with the exception of offensive messages or images on clothing. In the private school both boys and girls wore a uniform of permissible styles and colors, and with no logos or words. Teachers were required to dress neatly and men had to wear dress shirts and ties.

The commute was shorter, but much more hectic. I had looked forward to being able to sleep in, but discovered if I did, traffic slowed me down considerably because I had to cross the Tacoma Narrows Bridge (when there was only one) along with thousands of other city-bound cars. Most of the vehicles, like me, had only one occupant – sort of like every ant heading to the anthill at once. To avoid the jam-up, I'd have to be on the bridge two hours before traffic built to a snail's pace and school started. As it turned out, I needed this time to keep up with correcting and recording homework.

One morning I encountered a dump truck stopped mid-bridge with its dump bucket up, and on my way home one afternoon, the car in front of me on the bridge slammed on its brakes because it was following the car in front of it too closely, and it managed to do a 180-degree, spin out, and ended up facing the wrong way. Amazingly, traffic in both directions managed to stop while the wrong-way-facing vehicle turned around to face the right direction.

The daily routine in each classroom began with roll call, then in the next five minutes a Bible verse was read by me or a student followed by a brief discussion, and any prayer requests.

Every Wednesday there was a chapel service with singing, a speaker or a presentation by classes, and prayer. This served as a break from daily classwork and was usually something to look forward to.

On most Friday afternoons there were pep assemblies for the various athletic teams. The cheer squad was especially well coached and even won awards in cheer leading competitions. These Christian school cheer leaders were professional looking in their performances, making every pep assembly worth attending.

Supervision of students at football games was sometimes required during the season, reminding me of my early days of supervising in public high school.

Sometimes, because my free period fell at the end of the day, during a time that another teacher had an appointment or couldn't be in their class, I would have to fill in for them. This was somewhat annoying, especially when I filled in for a gym class, and had to run around in my street clothes with a whistle in my mouth.

In the spring the high school's students and teachers spent three days and two nights at a "retreat" in a camp area in the "boonies" in barracks, for a time of bonding and activities away from school. The experience was worthwhile in that we could see how individuals behaved outside of a classroom.

Also, once a year the school's staff would attend a Christian Conference in Portland, Oregon where we would share a motel room with two or more staff members. We attended various workshops/lectures based on Christian principles while meeting with other Christian school staff members from Washington, Oregon and Idaho. This also proved worthwhile and enjoyable break from teaching.

Staff meetings were sometimes a letdown as far as solving student behavior situations. The school's budget was based on how many students enrolled. This wasn't a problem in the established grade school and junior high school, because most of these students started in this school early on, and continued until they had to attend high school. But with the starting of a high school at the church facility, we newly-hired high school teachers had to attract and keep students who probably were attending or thinking of attending other high schools. As it turned out, some of the transfer students would be attending our school because they weren't doing so well in their current school. Classroom disrupters were a challenge because they were paying to go to school, and unlike public school, disrupters couldn't just be dropped or transferred to another class because of misbehavior. For example, I was *the one and only* English teacher, and since English is required to graduate from any high school, the student would have to attend another institution in order to take the required class. I actually refused to allow one of my continually misbehaving students, whose father was a pastor in another church, to be in my classroom. This student ended up attending summer school in order to receive credit, and returned to my English class the following year with a cooperative attitude.

In the nearly three decades of teaching in public school, seldom did I have to contact a student's parent or guardian about their student's classroom performance. I felt sorry for those teachers that turned in piles of referrals on a regular basis. Now, I was getting a taste of their experience.

The first assignment given in each of my classes was EXPECTATIONS which had to be signed by the student and their parent/guardian.

Name_____ Period_____

Mr. Edgers'

EXPECTATIONS

There will be a variety of assignments that will need to be done in order to receive credit and a grade in

_____ (this class)

Punctuality will be stressed, and late assignments will be noted

Daily Assignments – notes, worksheets, rough drafts, reports, reading, etc.

Major Assignments – Research papers and other <u>written assignments</u> will be judged on neatness, organization, thought, effort, spelling, grammar and originality.

<u>Oral Assignments </u>will be judged on organization, thought, effort, originality and style of presentation.

Quizzes – small amounts of information, vocabulary, etc.

Tests – major amounts of information (usually notes may be used)

Some Activities and Assignments will not relate to the specific class in which the student is enrolled, but rather deal with learning and self-improvement techniques such as, <u>how to:</u> listen better, study more effectively, improve memory, develop a larger vocabulary, set goals and be more successful.

Extra Credit – Assignments turned in early (before a deadline) – typed assignments – audio/video/multimedia skits or similar presentations relating or pertinent to a topic studied in the subject are encouraged.

Suggestions/Comments:

Student Signature _____

Parent/Guardian Signature _____

Date this assignment was turned in _____

Problem students were identifiable early in the school year, but when we had faculty meetings the high school's principal advised us to keep tabs on the disrupters and try to get them on the right track. One principal's MEMO phrased it this way: "This 'incident' (alcohol-related) is to be considered that—an incident and not a lifestyle habit. Please do not label these students as 'bad' kids but instead pray for them and support them."

Three weeks into the year, four students were suspended for three days and placed on behavioral probation for one month because of being involved in an alcohol-related incident. A month later we received notice that five students were suspended for three days and two of the "behavioral probation" students from the "alcohol related incident" were "no longer attending."

Besides my EXPECTATIONS I had another ½ slip of paper like a referral (in my public school) that suspended a student from my class until one of their parents/guardians met with me concerning one or more classroom behavior problems: Disruptions – Rudeness – Disrespect – Interfering with the teacher's right to teach or students' right to learn – Not doing assignments – Wasting time – Continuing to talk when asked to be quiet – Vandalism – Other

The lowest grade level I had taught in my previous high school (10th, 11th and 12th grades) was Sophomore English. I considered 10th graders immature, but teachable once they realized high school was different than junior high school in what was expected of them (sometimes referred to as 'whipping them into shape.')

So, when I had two classes of 9th graders, I was apprehensive of what to expect. Fortunately, one of these classes was 'super-duper' and took to learning English like ducks to water. Then there was their antitheses at the end of the day that drove me up the wall.

For example, there was one boy in my 6th period freshman English class that absolutely went out of his way to attract attention to himself and distract the class' attention from me e.g. crawl from the back of the room to the front. When his mother came in to see me, she refused to believe her son would do such a thing, and insinuated that I was a liar. I had an elderly assistant who helped me with paperwork after school sitting at my desk across the room where the disbelieving mother and I were talking who piped up, "I was here and saw your boy do exactly what Mr. Edgers described. And I've seen him misbehave several other times."

This boy wasn't the only student who wore me out with his behavior in my 6th period freshman English class. If I didn't know better, I'd suspect they were on pep pills and had ants in their pants. It was like trying to gain control over an octopus with an uncontrollable itch. The majority of the class was the most immature group of students I has ever run across in 29 years. I had to post the following:

RULES FOR 6TH Period FRESHMAN ENGLISH

Because of the number of students who arc **loud, disruptive, rude** and/ or **otherwise wasting my time** and **other students' time**, I am going to impose the following **rules in order to restore order and a good learning environment to this class:**

> I will videotape each classroom session in order for you to see and hear what I see and hear from the time you enter the classroom until the end of the period, in order to document your behavior.

DO NOT TOUCH THE VIDEO EQUIPMENT AT ANY TIME!

<u>THE FOLLOWING IS EXPECTED OF EACH STUDENT</u>:

1. Go to your seat/desk without pushing, shoving or in any other way disturbing any other student.

2. You may **<u>visit quietly</u> until the bell rings.**

3. **<u>Do not talk</u> at all <u>while I take roll</u>** (after the bell)

4. Get out books, pens/pencils, papers, <u>quietly</u> for the day's assignment. (Use your Student Planner and call the *Trib(une)* Line to write down and do the next day's assignment and bring the correct book we'll use.)

5. You have enough time between classes to use the restroom, get a drink of water or go to your lockers. **Do not ask to leave the classroom (unless it is an emergency).**

6. When I am talking to the class, I expect <u>**you**</u> to follow the <u>Six Guides to Better Listening</u> which are:

    - **L**ook at me.
    - **A**sk Questions (after my explanation, if you do not understand.)
    - **D**on't interrupt.
    - **D**on't change the subject
    - **E**motions (control them)
    - **R**esponsive (give feedback to show you are listening).

7. <u>Stay in your seat</u> for the entire period unless I ask you to turn in a paper or I ask you to give me an assignment. (Sharpen pencils before class starts).

8. <u>Do not throw anything, ever!</u> Put trash or other throwaway material in the wastebasket <u>after </u>class.

9. <u>Do not bring or consume any food (candy included) or beverage </u>into the classroom.

10. Please speak to me in a normal tone of voice!

11. Treat others the way you would like to be treated.

If you continue to cause problems and don't behave as a high school student or any other human being, you may be dealt with by the school's administration. Each violation (infraction) will be noted, and I will call your parent(s)/guardian(s) concerning your behavior and performance.

MY JOURNAL ENTRIES FROM 1995 to 1997

The following entries may sound like the spiritual *Nobody Know the Trouble I've Seen,* or Tommy LaSorda's (LA Dodgers' manager) comment, "I found out it's not good to talk about my troubles. Eighty percent don't care and twenty percent are glad you're having them."

<u>Sept. 12, 1995</u> The fourth day of teaching went O.K., but I had to stay in my room at lunch to try finishing up correcting of English papers. I still didn't get done and had to continue into the beginning of 6th period in order to get them all corrected.

I wonder if I'm being punished or being hardened by God. Some of my students this year are sorely-testing me. Sometimes I feel like I'm invisible because my words are swallowed by noise or confusion. I want to teach subjects and information and help students think and learn, but some obviously don't care about anyone but themselves and don't care if they drag down anyone around them.

<u>Sept. 13, 1995</u> Open House (back to school night) on Monday really wiped me out. I'm still not back to strength. I noticed in the Faculty Bulletin that it's recommended that I go to a Wednesday night class here called *Roots & Wings* which tells me about the history and philosophy of this particular church. It should be interesting, but with the Back to School Night and all, I know it will probably wipe me out again. Oh well, the weekend is not too far off!

I can really notice the difference in maturity between the juniors, sophomores and freshmen, although I do have a group of freshmen who are quite mature and manage, despite their classmates, to do very well in their class. No doubt, many students will look back on their freshman and sophomore years and wonder how they could've behaved the way they did.

<u>Sept.14, 1995</u>   I went to a class called *Roots & Wings* last night, and was a little disappointed with it because it's aimed at new Christian believers, so the information was really pretty basic. The teacher would whip over some of the information so fast toward the end of class that

I'm sure many people don't have a clue as to what the guy said. It's too bad,

Sept.15, 1995   I'm having some stress over my 6th period freshman English class because of the attitude (negative) and behavior (rowdy) of a few of them. When I'm taking role, it's a lot like a group of first graders on a playfield. They all are practically shouting at each other, yet only two or three feet separate them. I'll get them quiet, and within a few seconds it sounds like a riot in the zoo! Unfortunately, some of them are borderline vandals and will try to do stuff like take things off the bulletin board, and I'm missing a tie tack that I like and I've had for many years, but I didn't get it back.

Oct. 2, 1995 Try as I might, I'm not enjoying teaching at a private school. I have the nicest room I've ever had, new updated text books, and the staff and faculty are great. However, there's more to teaching than those things. The key ingredients (motivated and teachable students) are missing.

I spend most of my weekends correcting papers or preparing lessons, but when Monday comes the students are rude, loud, uncaring and misbehave. It's almost like they're on a mission to defeat me.

I don't want to bash my brains out doing something I actually loved doing, and then on Monday feel like a prisoner in my classroom. My stomach is in a continual knot and I feel overwhelmed.

Oct.5, 1995 *Letter* given to high school administrators:

October 5, 1995 – 2:10 AM

Dear (administrators),

I thought I'd jot down the above time so that you can see school is on my mind at all times of the day and night.

I left school 12 ½ hours after arriving yesterday, and was able to get home relatively early for a Wednesday (church activity) night as my *Roots & Wings* class was over an hour earlier than the three previous classes.

I headed to McDonald's to get a bite to eat because I got so engrossed in grading papers after school that I lost track of **time** and missed the (complimentary) Family Dinner before my Wednesday night class.

After our All Staff Meeting yesterday, I was talking with the junior high English teacher to see how he was doing with his classes, and found that he is swamped with assignments to read, grade and get into his grade book. I have the advantage of having no children to raise and a wife willing to help me keep up with putting grades in my grade book, where (the JHS English teacher) doesn't. It became clear that he and I need **assistance**, and we need it **now!** We could keep an aide busy six hours a day, five days a week for the rest of the year. Since school has started, I have not had a free day on any weekend because of the amount of paperwork the English classes generate, plus I'm trying to keep up with three different grade levels using new materials (to me) in those classes. To make matters worse, I have one large class that has (as you know) some students that have behavior problems. My wife says, "Just write them up and get rid of them! Nobody should have to put up with that type of student!" The problem is I just don't have **time!** I don't have time to write them up or call their parents, or for that matter, figure their grade average or fill out their report cards. Most days I get to school before 6:30 AM and leave after 3:30 PM, eat dinner, take a walk, and do schoolwork until 9:30 or 10:00. Throw in *Roots & Wings,* Back to School Night, or any other afterschool activity, and I get behind because there just aren't enough hours in the day without **assistance!** I've had to resign from all my community and church activities because I no longer have **time** for them.

I have three different literature books to read so I can prepare lessons for that part of the English classes. Then there are two different writing books which obviously generate writing assignments. Plus there are quizzes, tests, essays and other papers to be corrected or graded or noted to be entered into a grade book. Now, I've done this all before, but the big difference between *then* and now is I had **assistance** then, and *now* I don't.

Please hire a language arts teacher's aide!

(Finished typing: 3:55 AM)

<u>Oct. 24, 1995</u>   I got up feeling depressed about the behavior of my 4th period drama class, 5th period sophomore English and 6th period freshman English classes. The drama class is splitting into a positive and negative attitudes. The negative are whining, moping and not participating or else they're doing work for other classes. The positive are trying to carry the negative, and it's a struggle. I'm trying to get them to write and adapt skits that are Christian oriented for Chapel, but they lollygag around, eat their lunch (which I've told them many times not to do) and waste the time. Suggestions are treated like garbage.

<u>Oct. 25, 1995</u>   [An unsent letter of discontent]

Dear (high school administrators),

I really appreciate the hiring of an outside teacher's aide, as she has proven herself a wonderful help. She has restored a semblance of normalcy to my life by taking away the overwhelming burden of paperwork. I am now able to spend time on reading ahead in the literature assignments.

One might feel that the joy of teaching would return to me and that the knot in my stomach would disappear. I'm still waiting for that to happen, and every day I come to school raring to go and to inspire my students and help them to be encouraged and challenged by the courses I teach. Every day by fourth period I run into a wall of mean spiritedness, negativity, disrespect and borderline chaos. I just don't get it! I have the feeling that I've lost touch with reality, and that I'm being punished for something. Sometimes I think to myself, "What did I do to deserve this?" and feel the knot of frustration tighten in my stomach.

(Vice principal friend) You gave such a rosy report on how great it was to teach in a Christian school compared to public school, and I couldn't quite imagine how I could enjoy it any more than I enjoyed teaching in public school. I absolutely **loved** teaching in public school, where I had virtually no behavior problems or had to send home disciplinary reports.

Just when I feel that I've got a handle on teaching, I get a snide remark from one student, an insanely loud disruption from another or a poorly written anarchist-type note* from still another.

10/25 * Student's note $

Mr. Edgers,

I'm not writing you this note to be disrespectful by any means, but I would like to say I have ~~to~~ talked to basicaly (sic) every student in your 10th grade English class, and every one (sic) agrees we are not really learning any thing (sic) in here,(sic) We would really apreciate (sic) learning grammer (sic), lit., spelling, and (sic) vocabulary, ect. (sic), instead of the stuff we are learning, that is usualy (sic) taught in self help (sic) classes (goals & stuff)

Most Sincerly (sic)

(Girl Student)

Oct. 26,1995   My response

Dear (Girl Student)

Sometimes you and I need a break in the subject matter, and in fact, the Headmaster suggested I use this (self-help) material with my classes. If the information was useless or merely for entertainment, I would tend to agree with you, but someday (if not now) the information I give you on Wednesdays may benefit you a great deal. If you have been listening in your Bible class, you may realize that your attitude toward something can make a big difference. If you try to have an open mind to new information you might benefit from it. For example, I did a unit on

"*How to Listen More Successfully*", which, as was pointed out, is a vital skill about which most people never learn. If you followed the steps that were laid out you might realize why you aren't a good listener. When you talk (as you do frequently) or distract others when I am giving important information, you are depriving yourself and those who are sitting near you of information that might be necessary to do well in the class. Also, poor listening is a rude habit, and doesn't do you any good.

Perhaps you should back off about telling me what I should or shouldn't do. Take a moment to think about how you behave and what you add or subtract from the class' attitude. Are you contributing to the class? Are you doing your job as a student? Or, are you being a "pain" or a heckler? If you've been paying attention, you may notice that I try to do my job as a teacher. I present information, correct papers and try to help you do better. If you acted like you wanted to improve and/or benefit from what information I give you, and then turned in near-perfect papers showing skill and insight, I would give some credence to your note.

If "everyone is not learning anything in here", they definitely have a learning problem that stems from a listening problem.

Mr. E.

P.S. If you or the other 10th grade students who are "learning nothing in here" on Wednesdays would like to meet with me after school on Wednesdays, I will gladly give you writing or literature or grammar lessons in order to give you your money's worth.

Oct. 27, 1995   The topic for chapel today was "Respect." The main point was to leave people more alive than when you found them. The three problem girls in my sophomore English class were there, but it didn't "take" as none of them did what they were supposed to do.

(It turned out that two of them were kicked out permanently for getting caught drinking alcohol during lunchtime, and the third was later kicked out of my class for the remainder of the year.) Some of the remaining class members quickly "got with the program" and the remaining part of the semester went a bit better. (I thought about Ezekiel 20:38 – "I will purge rebels from among you –")

Oct. 31 – Nov. 30, 1995 There are still problem students – mainly in 6th period freshman English, so I submitted the following letter: $

November 30, 1995

Dear (High school Administrators)

I am finishing three months in the classroom, during which time I have experienced about one month of relief in work load because of (English aide). However, I am once again getting a sinking feeling as we approach the end of the semester, not because of the work load, but rather because of the ongoing, uphill battle with behavior-problem-students who continue to plague my classes. I fill out forms on the worst of the problem students, but absolutely nothing happens, which, in turn, effects the behavior of the borderline problem student, clear down to the normally well behaved student. The bad apples are still here even after the meeting we had identifying those "apples" two months ago. The teacher input obviously hit deaf ears. **Now hear this!** I am no longer filling out reports and calling parents. This is above and beyond the job I was hired to do. Once I fill out a report, the student discipline is your job. One warning should be sufficient in private school as it is in public school. The students who have been removed from this school had one warning. Drugs and alcohol are no different in my mind than misbehavior in the classroom.

I was hired to teach, but I am also doing the job of a discipline-administrator. (This school's) students know nothing much will happen to them if they misbehave, are rude, defiant or commit acts that would not be tolerated in my classroom in public school.

With, what I perceive as ignoring my pleas for backup or reinforcement, you tell me, "You must be doing the wrong thing!" I'm not doing the wrong thing! I am a master teacher who's regularly undermined by students and the administration to the point that I feel like a whipping boy. I'm not being allowed to teach full-time because much of my time is taken up with discipline matters, and I'm getting tired of the same old "same-as-usual no action on discipline" routine.

Starting Monday (December 4th) if the same students I write up regularly have the same-as-usual misbehavior, I am sending them to the office to be removed from my class. If this seems unreasonable, so be it! It's either my way, so I can teach those who want to learn, or I'm through! The administrative inaction has so undermined me in the classroom that I'm dying as a teacher. The joy of teaching in a lackadaisically-administered school turns to anguish.

Next — One English/Language Arts teacher is not enough. I am being spread way too thin by having so many new (as in books to read and lessons to prepare) levels of English to teach, plus elective subjects where I have to improvise. Another teacher needs to be hired at the semester. If you want a quality school with quality programs you need adequate staff.

I would appreciate a response as soon as possible regarding the hiring of an additional high school English/Language Arts teacher for the coming semester.

Respectfully,
D. Edgers

December, 1995

Finally, my appeal didn't fall on deaf ears! I realized that the high school administrators had little or no experience at the high school level. The headmaster was a former athletic coach, but I don't know about any other school administration positions he may have had. The high school principal had experience as a classroom teacher up to 6th grade and previously was a principal at the pre-high school level. Both administrators came to their jobs not knowing what to expect from their students and teachers. Almost immediately, the headmaster came to my classroom containing my problem kids, lecturing them on shaping up, or facing the consequences from him. His bearing and reputation as a coach made this forceful warning meaningful and affective. Most of my problems disappeared.

<u>1996</u> Beginning the second semester, another English teacher was hired to take my 9th and 10th grade classes and I taught speech, junior English, junior high school keyboarding and word processing on small word processors called Dream Writers®, and assisted in the computer lab. My morale increased greatly.

At a Teachers' Weekly Devotion class where we studied a Christian book appropriately aimed at teachers, and had sort-of pep talks or presentations by faculty, I was asked to speak and tentatively titled my talk: *"The Lord works in mysterious ways His wonders to perform – Teaching an old dog new tricks aka Have faith and hang on!*

I told of my struggles with my time and students at the high school, even with 28 years of high school teaching behind me. I pointed out other experiences throughout my life when I wondered if I was being punished or tested by God. I said, "I didn't think of it at the time of my troubles, but even the apostle Paul when he first went to Thessalonica got chased out of town by an angry mob. Through faith he persisted, and we can learn of the payoff in 1st and 2nd Thessalonians. (He had faith and hung on)."

<u>1996-1997</u> This school year is much less stressful because I teach 12th grade American literature/speech, Middle School speech/photography, drama/film study and worked in the computer lab. The only classroom I have with windows is one period when I get out of the basement to teach the 12th grade class.

<u>December,1996</u> I made a proposal to the School board pointing out the school's lack of computer technology, and compared coming from my former school as leaving a big vibrant technologically proficient city to a quaint village that just had gotten electricity. Unbelievably, the entire school had **one** Internet connection which was in the school's office – not in the computer lab.

A five page proposal for updating the computer lab with new hardware and software was presented. The need was understood and by spring the entire computer lab was in the middle of being rewired and connected to the world outside of the school.

<u>April, 1997</u> To Whom It May Concern:

I feel very fortunate to have been able to teach at this school for the past two years, and see God work miracles in many students' lives.

I have now reached the 30-year period in my teaching career, and feel that I have accomplished the plan God had for me as a full-time teacher. After considerable prayer, thought, debate and discussion, I have reached the decision to conclude my full-time teaching career in order to spend more time writing articles and books, and pursuing other activities.

This past year I have experienced the poorest health of my entire life which made me realize that there are other talents I haven't fully put to use. I suspect my poor health is related to such things as the lighting, unfiltered air, poor air circulation and other unhealthy conditions in the computer lab – and the hectic pace of a seven-period school day.

When I was in public school the hectic pace was relieved by going to longer and fewer periods with a four-period school day, which meant we only taught three periods a day. Many other schools are also doing this because it tends to lessen the stress for both teachers and students, plus less time is wasted taking roll, starting and stopping lessons. The six and seven-period day was decided on as the school day by five men over 100 years ago and is not practical or realistic for the 21st century. Using the Bible as an analogy, the seven-period day would be the King James Version, and the four-period day would be the NIV. I realized this school wouldn't be changing any time soon, at a recent two-hour after school faculty meeting when this topic was discussed and a faculty/administrator stated: "We more than likely won't go to fewer/long-length periods because the school board won't go for it, and frankly, I like a seven-period day!" (100-year-old paradigm?)

After the meeting I had to get in the bridge commuter traffic and spend 20-minutes longer than usual in traffic, then, after dinner, try to catch up on the two-hours of paper correcting that wasn't done because of the meeting.

I feel there are other signs I should conclude my full-time teaching career, like: moving me every period I teach; many requests for a book shelf to enable me to get my materials, books, folders, videos and films off the floor; a table; a desk with drawers – ignored the entire year. These serve as humbling and frustrating experiences.

If this school went to a four-period day, or I could teach a 3/7th day (three periods in a seven-period day), I would be open to that as an alternative to totally quitting (if the school wanted me to teach).

I thoroughly enjoy the students, faculty and staff and their dedication to Christian education. *Someday I hope to write about the experiences I've had during my tenure at this school,* but with the seven-period day, that wouldn't be an option unless I retire altogether.

Sincerely,
D. Edgers

SUBSTITUTE TEACHING

1997-1998 Honestly, I never thought I would succumb to pleas to teach as a substitute. But I was a natural choice because I knew all the kids I would be teaching, and it was a few extra dollars in my pocket. Also, I didn't have to go to meetings, grade papers, plan lessons, etc.

I only filled in for three or four different teachers, with one teacher who taught business classes occupying most of my time. He had kidney stones that kept him out for days at a time.

When another teacher asked me why the teacher I was substituting for was out, I mentioned his bout with kidney stones. She told me she had kidney stone troubles now and then saying, "I've gone through childbirth and kidney stones. I prefer childbirth."

TEACHING JUNIOR HIGH ENGLISH

January, 1998 When the second semester rolled around, the junior high
principal (the friend who talked me into teaching at the high school)
approached me to see if I would teach seventh and eighth grade English
for a quarter. The regular teacher had requested a sabbatical in order
to take some college classes that were only taught during the college's
winter quarter which would enable him to move up on the school's pay
scale.

The only time I had worked with that age group was during three
summers I drove a berry bus and was a field supervisor for a large berry
farm and the majority of the kids I picked up were junior high schoolers.
They were pretty squirrely as a whole, but I got along with them very
well. But remembering my days as a student in junior high school, I
couldn't imagine teaching short-attention-span, constantly moving
students. However, I knew most of these kids, and thought, "Why not?" I
dove into, what was to be, my last hoorah as a school teacher.

The students were friendly and respectful of me because they'd seen
me as a high school teacher. I suspect they knew they couldn't put
anything over on me. As I got a feel for my charges, it became apparent
they had a way to go before their brains functioned at a normal rate.
They would look at me with wide eyes when I told them what they
would have to know when they got to high school. It was like I told
them how to change lead into gold. I laughed every day at their actions
and words. For example, a seventh grade girl did something incredibly
"stupid" and when I asked her how she thought she could get away with
what she did, she replied, "Mr. Edgers I'm 12-years-old, and I've only
known the difference between right and wrong since I was 10." She
turned 13 a short time later and I told her, "Now that you're 13, *the Age
of Accountability*, you have no excuse." After my time in the classroom
with this age group, and the enjoyment of teaching them, I thought to
myself, "I think I could've taught junior high for all 30 years."

~20~

How I Became a Student in My Own House

My best laid plans (writing books) may have been set aside for two years, but they had not been forgotten. Our daughter was married and moved; our dog had chosen to live at our neighbor's; we sold our large house and built another home a little way down the road. All of this occurred during my private school teaching time. Out of all these events, the selling of our waterfront home was the most beneficial to my goal of writing a book.

The couple who bought our house moved from the city of Port Angeles to Fox Island, primarily so the husband, Charles Keim, a retired University of Alaska, Fairbanks, professor would have a peaceful setting that would allow him to concentrate on and finish writing an epic Western, *Little Coyote*, before he died of cancer.

As he knew nothing of the history of Fox Island, I provided several copies of historical articles I had written over the years for a local monthly publication. Upon reading the articles, the former journalism and English professor asked me to come to his "new" house to discuss them. He asked me what I planned to do with them – if anything. I had thought about putting the articles as written into one volume. He thought these articles could be worked into a story of Fox Island in the 1940s as seen through my eyes as a 10-year-old. Taking me under his wing as a student, he told me, "I'll make some suggestions and corrections to what you write, and you don't have to abide by them or look at them as criticisms.

So began our weekly sessions as student and teacher in what had been my former master bedroom – now-classroom – of my "old" house / his "new" house.

Usually, on a once-a-week schedule, I'd bring my new or reworked stories for my professor's perusal where he'd teach me how to really write for publication.

Also, during this time he sent his book to a publisher and I learned some valuable lessons about the publishing world. The publisher, located in Montana, made trips to Fox Island, to meet with my teacher in order to discuss editorial and other pre-publishing material. I was privy to listen-in to their exchanges. This was valuable information I probably couldn't have learned in any other classroom.

Professor and close friend, Charles Keim, passed away in 1998, two years after his final book was published and four years before I finished writing *An Island in Time: Growing up in the 1940s.* That book was followed by *AN ISLAND IN TIME II: Coming of age in the 1950's* (2007) and *Fox Island* (2008).

I feel extremely blessed to have been born where, when and to whom I was with the genes and proclivities that steered me into the field of education. Hopefully, my experiences have benefitted and encouraged most of those who entered my realm.

I would encourage others who wonder what their life is all about to follow the adages:

- Bloom where you're planted.

- Make the best of what you've got.

- If you are or will be a teacher, teach others the way you would like to be taught.

~Don Edgers~

AFTERWORD

AWARDS/HONORS

Using food as an analogy, I would equate
awards or honors as icing on a cake.

- The North Kitsap Auxiliary 2463 branch of the Veterans of Foreign Wars of the United States presented me with Award Citations for providing Voice of Democracy speakers for state speechwriting contestants from my speech class students.

- Six senior classes voted to have me as a Commencement Speaker, starting in 1975.

- North Kitsap S.D. Indian Education Program Outstanding Teacher for the High School – 1983-84.

- Petitions from teachers and students asking me to return to school after I walked out

- 25-Year Service Pin and Certificate.

- A plaque of appreciation for 28 years of service in the school district.

- A framed letter from the White House congratulating me on "many rewarding years in the field of education." It was signed (or rubber-stamped) by President Bill Clinton.

- A mounted and framed humorous painting of a classroom full of mostly misbehaving cartoon animals, with the teacher depicted as an owl, titled 'the learning experience.' An attached placard says, "Don Edgers – North Kitsap High School – September 1967-June 1995."

<u>R.I.P.</u>

Miss Entz – Kindergarten

Col. Jacobson – High School Superintendent

Col. Hahn – High School Principal

"Major" Lilich – High School Tactical Officer

SFC Puhr – Military Science

Mrs. Cantrall – English & Speech teacher

'Tuna Ben' Slavin – Coach

Jamie Pierce – Roommate for four years in a military high school

~

Miss Ellis – High School V.P.

Robert Alford – School District Superintendent

Don Johnson – Counselor

Ken Sparrow – Counselor

Steve Tucci – Math

Les Backlund – Math

Martin Amundsen – English

Hope Wade – English

Sharon Ferguson – English

Janice Nelson – Secretary

Harry Sandberg – Woodshop

Ruth Nohel – P.E.

Fred A. - Custodian

Printed in the United States
By Bookmasters